Hunting Hollywood:
A Guide to Famous Filming Locations

Rick Garland

ISBN-13: 978-1506199719

ISBN-10: 1506199712

Dedicated to my beautiful wife Amy. Without her patience and navigation skills none of this would have been possible. Thank you for “Hunting Hollywood” with me. I love you.

Contents

Other Books by Rick Garland

Lessons From My Fathers
Joy to the World
Unholy Devotion (Booklet)
Understanding Believers Baptism (Booklet)

All titles available through

www.rickgarland.com

Introduction

Whenever I tell people my hobby of looking up and visiting filming locations the question naturally arises about how I got involved in such a hobby. The answer is simple, it came about by accident. I heard a rumor that the television show "Scrubs" which was a favorite of mine was filmed in an actual hospital and not in a studio.

I doubted this information and decided to look it up online. When it was confirmed that it was indeed filmed in a hospital building I thought it would be neat to visit that building and see it in person. My then girlfriend and I were wanting to go to Hollywood for the day anyway so we decided to hop a Greyhound from where we lived in Bakersfield and go to North Hollywood where the hospital was and then take the subway into Hollywood from there.

After this trip I was planning to take my sister and brother in law to Hollywood since she had never been there. I wanted to take them by that hospital but really wanted to make the trip special so I decided to see if any other shows were filmed nearby. I found a few and added them to our itinerary.

Once we returned home from the trip my sister was curious about other shows and found a few more locations in the Southern California area. This enticed me to look for yet others. Before long I not only had a good size list but I was planning a trip just to see these places that I had seen before only on television.

This first full sightseeing trip deepened my desire to find more and more places. Soon more and more trips followed usually trying to see 20 to 30 houses per trip. I then began to go back and see places more than once as I took several friends on trips to see some of these places. I present here pictures from the shows as well as pictures of my own. My pictures are on top and the ones from the show are on the bottom so you can compare them.

My love for television and movies or as I say "Classic Hollywood" goes back to being raised partially by my grandparents who instilled in me a love for the old black and white movies of the golden era of Hollywood. We watched on a regular basis movies from the 30's to the 60's and my love for the actors and actresses, clothing styles, and elegance of that era was forever sealed.

My first visit to Hollywood as a 13 year old boy even furthered my love. Seeing the tall buildings of Downtown Los Angeles, left me breathless. I was awestruck walking down Hollywood Boulevard looking at the stars names on the sidewalk. I was filled with wonder as I saw the old buildings that I just knew were used by the celebrities of days gone by.

I did not return for over 15 years but as an adult I was able to rekindle that awe. Even today though I have been to Hollywood at least 3 dozen times I walk the streets with awe and wonder. I can't pass the Taft building without picturing Clark Gable bursting through the doors to play cards in the basement during a break at the studio.

I can't sit in Musso and Frank Grill without picturing my favorite character actor William Frawley in there having his many meals and then tracing his steps back to the Knickerbocker Hotel where he lived for many years. I can't look at the Roosevelt Hotel without picturing Shirley Temple learning her now famous stair dance in the lobby or without picturing elderly resident Elizabeth Patterson returning home after shooting “I Love Lucy” at nearby Desilu Studios.

I know those days are long gone but when I walk the streets or drive around town I take myself back to a place where the Marx Brothers make us laugh, where Hope and Crosby are making Road Trips, where Jack Benny is guarding his beloved safe, and where the scheming Lucy is still trying to get into the show. Come with me as we take a journey from yesterday to today and see the filming locations of shows and movies we love.

Join me now in Hunting Hollywood!

Part 1:

Television Filming Locations

"Scrubs"

2001-2010

Unfortunately I discovered this show after it was well underway and had to catch up. The show takes place in a hospital called Sacred Heart Hospital and centers around the careers of interns, residents, and attending physicians. The Janitor plays a major role as does the hospital lawyer and several nurses. The show was a masterful blend of comedic genius and heartwarming genuineness.

Dr. Kelso is the Chief of medicine who enjoys tormenting the hospital lawyer who lacks common sense, people skills, and knowledge of the law. Dr. Cox is the ego-centric attending physician who lives to torment the residents and interns who begin their career at Sacred Heart. The only person who can control him is Carla, a nurse whom everyone respects, and Cox fears. She marries Chris Turk the resident surgeon who has a tough exterior but a childlike alternate personality.

He is best friends with Dr. Dorian, a needy resident who craves the approval of Dr. Cox and often gets into private battles with The Janitor who is known for most of the series by that name. It has been his personal goal to make Dr. Dorian suffer since an unpleasant interaction between them in the first episode.

Dr. Reed rounds out the main cast as a spoiled rich girl who suffers from major personality disorders and though just as needy for approval as Dr. Dorian she attempts to mask it by putting forth a strong personality. Many other characters are involved in the show and each contribute in a major way to the charm and humor that made this show such a hit.

Rick Garland

It was watching Scrubs that gave me the desire to work in a hospital which I did for 6 years after first watching the show. When I first heard that the show was filmed in an actual abandoned hospital I knew I just had to see it in person. When you watch a show or movie you come to terms with the fact that it is fiction but when you get the chance to visit the place in person it gives the show a bit more reality.

I found out that the show was filmed at the former North Hollywood Medical Center. The hospital opened in 1952 as Valley Doctors Hospital containing an E.R. and 160 beds. In the early 1970's the hospital was known as Riverside Hospital. In 1981 a man who worked as a nurse there killed patients in Riverside County. The killings were not related to Riverside Hospital but to avoid the negative association they changed the name to Medical Center of North Hollywood. Due to financial struggles the Hospital closed in 1998.

This is a view of the Hospital during my visit there in 2011. When watching the show I always noticed it appeared to be on a busy street and indeed it is. One interesting fact is that most of the filming was done within a few blocks of the hospital. I will chronicle some of those places in this book as well.

The building was used for a number of productions but is best known and recognized for its time as Sacred Heart. Nearly all of the sets used on “Scrubs” (including the apartments) were filmed on the hospital property since only a few areas were used for the actual hospital set. We could not access the back parking lot where much of the shooting took place unfortunately.

The next picture is of the main driveway leading back to that area. This was the ambulance entrance during the time this was a regular hospital. If you look in the distance you can see the hedge of bushes and trees between the parking lot and the canal in the background.

These trees served for many of the parking lot sequences in the show. The rear entrance to the building was the primary door used when the cast would enter Sacred Heart. The front door was used primarily from the inside when someone would come in from the outside but was rarely seen used from the outside.

One of the problems that was faced by cast and crew was the issue of walk-in patients. The building looked like an up-and-running hospital. There were ambulances, people in wheelchairs and workers in scrubs. People often came in sick or injured seeking medical care. They had to be redirected to an actual hospital.

The picture below is most recognizable to me from a Season 5, episode where Dr. Dorian did not have his scooter and had to use a tiny scooter from a kid. In the scene he rides past the security guard's booth coming in from Riverside Drive. He grabs the newspaper from the security guard and keeps going. There is also a scene where Dr. Dorian gathers his interns outside the gate of the hospital. This area can be clearly recognized from that as well. The hospital was located at 12629 Riverside Drive in North Hollywood.

When it comes to the main hospital I really find it hard to say much about what has changed since unfortunately on my next trip it was already being torn down. I was so excited to take my sister and brother in law to see the famous "Scrubs Hospital" and then we turned the corner and my heart sank as we saw the building torn to its frame. Apparently when we had gone to the hospital the first time we got to see it just weeks before they began to tear it down. This was my last view of "Sacred Heart" before leaving that first visit.

You can imagine my surprise when I came back just weeks later and found the frame of this building with all walls, and windows removed. After some investigation I discovered that they were building apartments on the site. The building was not as nice as it appeared on television and was in a bad state of disrepair. I would rather them have opened it up for tours or something to give fans a chance to walk through the set where the show was filmed rather than to simply tear it down without warning.

In the years to come apartments will now stand where Sacred Heart Hospital once stood. These are the apartments under construction in 2013.

Other areas around the Hospital were used for filming. I have not been able to track them all down but I have included a number that I have visited. If you are looking to see where Scrubs was filmed you can still visit and recognize many of these locations.

I will refer to them all as North Hollywood but some may be officially Sherman Oaks, or Valley Village. The lines between towns are easily crossed but they are all within a mile or two of each other.

In the picture on the next page we see a street that was used in a scene from Season 2, Episode 1. In this episode J.D. and Turk were walking to work. It was filmed on Riverside Drive just up from Laurel Canyon Blvd. It's funny, I sat at the Starbucks at Laurel Canyon and Riverside once and had no idea I was 20 feet away from a Scrubs filming location.

The Chevron Station and green tarp over the building are visible in the show and are still visible as of this writing. Be cautious when looking for this place since it is on a very busy street.

PAT'S

The picture on the next page is from Season 2, Episode 15 where Turk proposes to Carla in the park. The filming location is Moorpark Park at 12061 Moorpark Street. I believe several episodes of Scrubs involving park scenes were filmed here but this is the only one I can say for sure.

The park is directly across the street from the apartment from the movie "The 40 Year Old Virgin." I recommend seeing both. The park is full of shade and beautiful trees. If you're looking for a nice picnic spot in the North Hollywood area then this would definitely be the spot.

One of my favorite parts of "Scrubs" was when they filmed on location. Much of the show's filming locations can be found all around the North Hollywood community. I have not been to all of them but as many as I could find.

I'll be honest this park wasn't even on my list. Finding it was sort of an accident for me. I came across it online just before my hunting trip and decided not to look for it because my plate was already full.

While getting a picture at the filming location across the street I turned around and there it was. This was my second time at this particular location but I guess the first time I didn't notice the park across the street.

The building on the next page is from season 2, episode 15 as well. This building can be seen in the scene where Turk proposes on top of the car as Elliot and Carla walk down the street. Dr. Dorian is next to the car with sparklers.

The building has changed slightly but is still completely recognizable and is directly across the street from the location of the hospital itself. It is on Riverside Drive but is at the corner of La Maida Street which dead ends into the building.

It dawned on me one day while watching the show that other buildings can be seen in the background. These would also count as filming locations and not just the building on which the episode focuses. I decided to find as many as I could.

This particular building being directly across from the hospital location can be seen in quite a few episodes. Once I started looking for it I was amazed at how many times I saw it pop up in the camera angles.

The only real change is the color of the building which was a dark brown but is now a much lighter color. Other than that it's pretty much the same. I tried my best to get a picture as close to the angle in the episode that I could.

KEY

The apartment building on the next page can be seen in Season 3, Episode 4. In this episode Dr. Dorian goes to Elliot's apartment and sees her crying through the window. The window faces the street so you can see it if you park directly in front of the building.

This particular location was used in multiple episodes. It can also be seen in Season 3, Episode 11. In this episode Dr. Dorian and Dani (Tara Reid) go to look at an apartment together.

In that particular episode I don't know how much of the building can be seen. They are pictured looking at the building so you can see behind them. The apartment is the Woodpark Apartments at 4424 Woodman Avenue in North Hollywood. **This is a private residence so please respect their privacy and do not trespass.**

When I took the picture I had forgotten which window she is seen in. I did remember which side so I just took a picture of that side of the apartment complex. Not much has changed since the show filmed here so it's pretty easy to recognize if you know what you're looking for.

ODPARK
4424

The house pictured on the next page took me a little while to nail down. It can be seen in Season 4, Episode 1. In this episode we see Dr. Dorian Picking up Carla's parents at the airport.

Instead of picking them up in a car like a normal person would do he picks them up on his scooter "Sasha." This location is visible only in passing as they ride down the street. If you're not watching carefully you will probably miss it.

You may not actually notice the house. What you can see in the episode is the black fence of this house as he drives by it. The house is located just around the corner from the old hospital site. Interestingly enough most of the house scenes were filmed on this street in close proximity to the rest of the set.

The house is located at 12737 La Maida Street. **This is a private residence so please respect their privacy and do not trespass.** When I was there the black fence was still around the house.

In one scene from Season 4, Episode 2, Dr. Dorian helped movers move into a house. It's actually a very funny scene as he is encouraging himself while he tries to lift furniture. In the scene, you don't see the actual house only the driveway.

It seemed like an impossible house to find since the front is never shown. I figured at first that it was simply filmed on site at the hospital. I knew I was wrong when I realized you can see other houses in the background.

I decided it must be a house and determined to find it. Once I realized their pattern for using houses on this street near the hospital it seemed logical it was there. It's so close in fact, the former hospital site can be seen from the house itself.

It is located at 12730 La Maida Street in North Hollywood. **This is a private residence so please respect their privacy and do not trespass.**

Home
for sale

The house on the next page was used in Season 5, Episode 13. It was one of the easiest for me to find. In this episode Dr. Kelso recalls his dad leaving the family on his bicycle.

In the scene The Janitor asks him why he hates bikes so much. Kelso thinks back to when he was a boy and his dad left his family on a bike. His dad assured him that since the car was in his mother's name he would not be able to leave the family forever were it not for Kelso's bike.

This particular episode called “My Five Stages” is one of my favorites. Kelso refuses to give Ted time off of work to bicycle for charity. This interaction is what leads us to the bicycle flashback for Kelso.

The house that was used is still a very recognizable bright yellow and is located just around the corner from the old Hospital site at 12733 La Maida Ave. in North Hollywood. **This is a private residence so please respect their privacy and do not trespass.**

The picture on the next page is the Colorado Street Bridge in Pasadena, California. This bridge has been used in probably countless movies and television shows over the years. I wish I had a list of all of them.

I will admit it wasn't easy to find. I circled Pasadena several times trying to find it. It's easy to get caught up in traffic which makes it hard to slow down to look for something.

The bridge can be seen in Season 2, Episode 7. In this episode Dr. Dorian and Elliot bungee jump off the bridge at Elliot's urging. Dr. Dorian is troubled that he does not take any risks in either his professional or private life.

The episode is called "My First Step." Heather Locklear makes a special guest appearance. During the episode each of the cast members seem to deal with taking risks.

Dr. Dorian, in regards to both his personal life and his career. Carla opposes going to nurse practitioner school because she is daring enough to place all of her efforts into her relationship with Turk. This is a daring decision that obviously pays off.

The exterior of Sacred Heart for the show in general was where they filmed at the former North Hollywood Medical Center. This was not the building used in the pilot episode. In many shows they use a different exterior for the pilot episode.

For "Scrubs" the hospital used in the exterior shots during the pilot was the Women's and Children's Hospital of Los Angeles. This is quite a distance from the hospital seen in the majority of the episodes. It is a much larger hospital than the one used for filming.

I tried as hard as I could to find the front doors shown on the episode but failed every time. If it's there then it's hidden well from sight. It's also possible the front was altered for television.

The building still looks exactly as it did in the show. If you're a fan of the show then I recommend seeing this building in the absence of the actual Sacred Heart building.

The hospital is at 1240 N. Mission Road in Los Angeles. I hope to continue finding and visiting Scrubs locations but as they say... I'm no superman.

"The Brady Bunch"

1969-1974

I think nearly everyone in America is familiar with the Brady Bunch. The show is to this day an ideal picture of the 1970's. Guest stars made up some of the most memorable episodes. There were stars such as Don Drysdale, Davy Jones, Desi Arnaz Jr. and Joe Namath just to name a few. The show was based on a widowed father of three boys named Mike Brady. Mike is an architect and his sons, Greg, Peter, and Bobby like their lives as four bachelors and are none too thrilled to join a new family. Mike also has a live-in housekeeper named Alice Nelson and the boys have a dog named Tiger.

Mike marries Carol Ann Martin (maiden name Tyler) who has children of her own. She has three blonde-haired daughters, Marcia, Jan, and Cindy. The show's creator Sherwood Schwartz wanted Carol to be divorced but he faced strong objections from the network so as a compromise they left her past open. It is not stated whether she is widowed or divorced.

The show's pilot depicts a very chaotic backyard wedding in which the two families become one. Each episode deals either with trouble between the two families as they learn to love each other, teen issues, sibling rivalry, or young love. The end of each episode usually has a very strong message of love, forgiveness, character, integrity or some other character trait.

The family lives in a large two story house that was supposed to have been designed and built by Mike himself and is located in Los Angeles. I grew up as a child in

Redwood City, California. We were surrounded by green foothills which always reminded me of the background for the Brady house. As a kid, I imagined that they lived in my town and would often keep my eyes out for the Brady house as we drove around town. You can imagine the thrill I had when I finally got to visit the Brady house in person.

The show was (as far as I know) the first of its kind which dealt with the issues of blended families. The pilot was shot in 1968 which ironically was the year that "Yours, Mine and Ours" starring Henry Fonda and Lucille Ball was released. The Brady script pre-dated the movie script so it was not based on the movie but the success of the movie did help.

The idea came to Sherwood Schwartz after he read in the L.A. Times that 30% of marriages have a child or children from another marriage. He wrote a script for a show he intended to call "Mine and Yours" but we know it today as "The Brady Bunch." To this day I love to watch "The Brady Bunch" not just for the memories of childhood but a fondness for Mike's soft fatherly advice, the quick wit of Alice and the many memories we shared with the children as we laughed, cried, feared, and rejoiced right along with them.

Who can forget the orange kitchen, brick oven, and brown wood that was so prevalent in the 1970's? How about the sliding glass door to the back patio and detached garage? Who remembers the long straight stairway with the thick heavy carpet? We can't forget to mention the AstroTurf in the backyard, or the swing set and teeter-totter. Then for me personally there is the opening sequence that shows the outside of the house and the rolling green foothills in the background which takes me back to the city of my youth.

We will start from the very beginning with this one. The picture on the next page is the house that was used in the pilot episode. This was Mike Brady's house.

In reality not much has changed over the more than 40 years since the episode was filmed. This house is located in a quiet and beautiful community. I have been to it on several occasions.

When visiting the house use consideration and common sense. The street is a regular area for walkers and runners. On my visits here I have seen regularly 20 or 30 people out and about so drive with caution and respect those who live in the area.

The house is located in Studio City, at 12049 Iredell Street. **This is a private residence so please respect their privacy and do not trespass.**

Rick Garland

The property pictured on the next page is also from the Brady Bunch pilot episode. It is unfortunate but the house is not very visible from the street due to a large wall that surrounds the house. This was Carol's parent's house where the wedding took place.

This house is only 3 to 5 miles from the house that was Mike's house in the pilot. The close distance makes them good to visit together. From what you can see of the house it is pretty much the same as when filming took place.

The backyard where the ceremony took place is not visible from the road. It can be seen online with an aerial view of the house. The stonework on the house is by far the most recognizable part of the house and the front door which was used in the episode is pretty clear from the road looking through the front gate.

Please do not try to climb the wall or invade the privacy of the residents. The house is located at 4101 Longridge Ave. in Sherman Oaks. If you visit this house please admire and enjoy all you can see from the road only. **This is a private residence so please respect their privacy and do not trespass.**

We now move on to the most notable and well known image that we remember from the Brady Bunch and that is the house that was used as the exterior for the Brady house in all of the episodes. This is probably one of the most famous houses in America and for years throughout the 1970's it was a stop for many visiting California.

The house was built for the original owner's because the house they were living in was destroyed by the Ventura Freeway construction. That information is kind of ironic when you consider the house was in danger of being destroyed by a freeway in an episode of The Brady's from the early 1990's. I believe those episodes were made into a movie but I'm not positive.

The house in the show was a large 2 story, 5 bedroom home but the house in reality was a very modest split level home. Production crews solved this problem by placing a fake window to give the allusion of a full second story. You will notice in the pictures that the window seen on TV over the left side of the house is not there today because it was not real.

The house was seen in many opening sequences from different angles either as just the front by itself, or with a car pulling in the driveway. We also see day and night photos of the house. These were all filmed before the series started and were used over and over throughout the show.

The house was sold in 1973 and as far as I know the

current residents have been there since. They don't mind the lookers who come by to see the "Brady House" but due to some people coming onto the property and trying to look in the windows a large gate has been put in front of the home. This gate does not obstruct the view of the home but reinforces the need to be respectful.

The address for the house is 11222 Dilling Street in Studio City. **This is a private residence so please respect their privacy and do not trespass.**

In the picture below you can see the wooden area where the false window was in the television show. I personally think it looks better without the window but the window did make the house look bigger.

In the picture below you can see the detached garage which is neat because the studio set depicted a detached garage. In fact from the street a look at the Brady driveway might convince someone that they actually filmed the episodes here.

Most of the scenes were filmed on the Paramount studios backlot such as the scene with Greg smoking by the tree. The tree is still there today though very withered. The school the older kids attended, as well as the ghost town the gang visited. These are all on the studio backlot. The parking lot where Greg and Marcia had their driving competition was also filmed at Paramount Studios.

Let's take some time now to view other filming locations from the Brady Bunch that were not filmed on the Paramount property. Some have changed considerably but you can still visit their former locations. I enjoy visiting locations even if the buildings have changed or have been torn down.

When you get to visit these locations it's like you're standing in a bit of history. It makes these shows seem more real, more tangible. We watched them as if they were real people and now we are standing where they stood.

In the picture on the next page we see Dixie Canyon Elementary School which was used as Cindy Brady's school in Season 1, Episode 3, “Eenie, Meenie, Mommy, Daddy.” The school is located at 4220 Dixie Canyon Ave. in Sherman Oaks, California.

DIXIE CANYON AVENUE SCHOOL

DIXIE CANYON

In the pictures below you can see Upper Franklin Canyon Reservoir which can be seen in Season 1, Episode 8 where the Brady clan goes camping. The lake was also used in the opening sequence of "The Andy Griffith Show."

In the picture on the next page you can see North June Street in Hollywood. This is where the Brady family was seen jogging in Season 3, Episode 20. This episode was called "Sergeant Emma."

Alice decides to take a vacation and calls her cousin Emma in to take her place. The problem is that Emma runs the household like an Army boot camp. The family soon has to find a way to get her to take a few days off so that they can get some rest.

The children are treated as privates in Emma's army and the parents fare slightly better as officers. The situation becomes tricky since she is Alice's cousin. The situation lends to many laughs and I suggest you see it if you haven't.

The scene was filmed in the neighborhood directly across the street from the Paramount Studio lot. The house they are passing in the picture is 101 N. June Street. **This is a private residence so please respect their privacy and do not trespass.**

On the next page is a picture from the same episode during Season 3 called, "Sergeant Emma." the Brady family can be seen jogging on West 1st Street and turning left onto Hudson Street. This was filmed on location in Hollywood.

Unfortunately at the time of the filming the area looked different. There were large trees, shrubs, and bushes blocking the view of the beautiful house on the corner. I think even the street light was changed or moved over a bit. The row of trees along the sidewalk and the sidewalk itself appear to be the most recognizable parts of the area.

The building that appeared as the outside of Mike Brady's office was the old Beverly Hills Library on Rexford Drive in Beverly Hills. The building was torn down and a new library stands in the same location.

The picture below was taken at Poinsettia Park at 7341 Willoughby Ave. in Los Angeles. This was the location from Season 2, Episode 16, where Peter got to play football with Deacon Jones.

In Season 2, Episode 15, Jan went to a shopping mall to buy a black wig in order to reinvent herself. The building used for the shots was the old Wilshire May Company building at 6067 Wilshire Blvd.

The picture below is a view of the front of the building. It really is a beautiful building. As a lover of the golden age of Hollywood I would have loved to see it in its prime.

In Season 3, Episode 8, the Brady family is discovered for a television commercial in the parking lot of a grocery store. The scene was filmed outside of what is today Gelson's Market located at 5877 Franklin Ave. in Hollywood. The brown building to the left of the market can be seen in the episode.

This building directly across the street from the market can be seen in the same episode while the family is talking to the director about doing a commercial.

In Season 3, Episode 13, Jan is seen riding her bike home. This was filmed on location in Hollywood. Jan is riding down N. Hudson and turns left onto W. 1st.

In Season 4, Episode 19, we see the family riding bikes through the neighborhood. This was filmed on location in Hollywood. They are riding on W. 1st Street passing Hudson. This has been the story of a man named "Brady."

"The Golden Girls"

1985-1992

There are not many people in the United States that can honestly say they have never heard of or watched "The Golden Girls." This show (which aired on NBC) is as close to an American icon as you can get. It is based on four single women who share a large home in Miami, Florida. The main storylines center on their desires to be rich and to find the right man or at least the wrong man if he is rich.

The home is owned by Blanche Devereaux played by Rue McClanahan. She is a widow who refuses to believe she is moving into the golden years of life. She works part time at a museum and spends the rest of her time chasing men.

Blanche is known for her numerous dates and seemingly embellished stories of her escapades with men. She rents the house to the other women for most of the show. She sells each of them a share of the house in Season 7, Episode 4.

One of her renters is Rose Nylund played by Betty White. Rose is originally from a strange little town called St. Olaf, Minnesota. St. Olaf is a town of dimwitted farmers who seem to only have good times even while marching with pitchforks.

Rose moves to Miami after the death of her husband, Charlie. She is known for her long, peculiar stories about her childhood and hometown. Rose is often heard saying strange things which many times lead to her roommates hitting her on the head with a paper. In later seasons she dated a college professor named Miles Webber quite regularly until it is revealed that his identity is a fraud and he is in the Witness Protection Program.

The next member of this odd quartet is Dorothy Zbornak played by Bea Arthur. Dorothy is a substitute teacher who divorced her husband Stan for cheating on her with a stewardess after 38 years of marriage. She became pregnant in high school which is why she married Stan, a fact her mother brings up continually.

Dorothy is from Brooklyn originally but she and Stan moved to Miami at some point in their marriage. Her father Sal is deceased but is seen in visions and flashbacks throughout the show. She had her mother Sophia put into Shady Pines, a low budget retirement home.

Dorothy has trouble with men and is mocked continuously for her lonely nights at home with a book. In the final episode she marries Blanche's uncle Lucas Hollingsworth. The two move to Atlanta, Georgia.

Sophia Petrillo rounds out the cast. She is played by Estelle Getty. Sophia is Dorothy's widowed mother who moves in with the other ladies when her retirement home Shady Pines burns down in the first episode.

Sophia is known for stealing from her daughter, and constantly trying to fix her up with any random man. She regularly surprises audiences with her tenacious attitude. She often tells stories that start with "picture this" and she usually turns out to be the subject of the story.

The concept of "The Golden Girls" actually came about quite suddenly in 1984. Selma Diamond of "Night Court" and Doris Roberts of Remington Steele did a parody of "Miami Vice" to advertise for the coming season. The parody was called "Miami Nice" and was about old people living in Miami. A network executive liked the idea of a show about older people.

He asked producers Paul Junger Witt, and Tony Thomas to come up with a "Miami Nice" script. Paul Junger Witt talked his wife Susan Harris into writing the script. This script was submitted to the network as "The Golden Girls."

In its original design, Rue McClanahan was cast as Rose and Betty White was cast as Blanche. McClanahan played a simple but sweet woman on "Maude," and White played a man hungry woman on "The Mary Tyler Moore Show." This led to them switching roles to keep from being typecast.

The chemistry was great because McClanahan had worked with Betty White on "Mama's Family" and with Bea Arthur on Maude. Estelle Getty who was actually younger than Betty White and Bea Arthur was a great addition to the cast because her character's age made the others seem young which helped with public appeal. Estelle Getty had to go through 3 hours of makeup, wear a white wig, and thick glasses to become the feisty Sophia.

An interesting note about the set of "The Golden Girls" is the kitchen from which many of the scenes originate. It was not created for this particular show. It was used in the show “It Takes Two” which aired from 1982 to 1983.

The kitchen set was saved when the show was canceled after only one season. It was brought back the same in 1985 for the first season of The Golden Girls and received only minor changes such as wallpaper after that. The other difference is the window view changed from Chicago buildings to palm trees for a Miami backdrop.

The outside shots of the famous house were shot in the Brentwood area of Los Angeles. The house with its greenery and palm trees was itself a picture of Florida. I never realized it was less than a handful of miles from the 405 Freeway.

Shots of the house were used in the first season. After the first season however, a duplicate was built at the studio. A house for Empty Nest which was a spinoff of The Golden Girls was also built in the studio.

In the picture on the next page, you see a view of the house, especially the driveway. You'll notice a difference in the front door. On the show it leads to an outdoor hallway but on the actual house it just opens outside.

On the show the patio is in back of the house and to the right of the door if you're inside the house. On the actual house it is to the left of the door from the inside and right next to the front door. In the storyline the house is a four bedroom, two bath. In reality, the house is a four bedroom, four bath.

In the picture below you see the plants and greenery that so famously told all of us that this house must be in Miami. These plants are probably some of the most recognizable landscaping in America or at least Southern California.

In the picture below you see the tall palm tree that is still standing and was the focal point of many of the opening sequences on "The Golden Girls." The house is located at 245 N. Saltair Ave. in Los Angeles. If you head west on Sunset Blvd. off the 405, make a right on N. Saltair Ave. Follow the street for less than half a mile and the house will be on your left. You should recognize it from pretty far away. **This is a private residence so please respect their privacy and do not trespass.**

It's time to move on now, but thank you for being a friend!

This is a view of the front of ***The Knickerbocker Hotel*** *in Hollywood. Actor William Frawley lived here for nearly 30 years and died in front of the hotel.*

"Happy Days"

1974-1984

This is a show that I know only from reruns as I was not born until 1981. The show is set in Milwaukee, Wisconsin and centers on the Cunningham family. The main character is the teenage son in the family named Richie (who is played by Ron Howard). The family consists of Richie's sister Joanie who is played by actress Erin Moran, his father Howard who is played by Tom Bosley, and his mother Marion who is played by actress Marion Ross.

Howard owns a hardware store and Marion is a traditional housewife. Other characters include Arthur Fonzarelli also known as The Fonze played by Henry Winkler. He is a high school dropout and ladies' man.

Fonzie is a biker and is made in the image of James Dean. In later episodes he moves into an apartment above the Cunningham's garage. Richie's friends were also major players in the show. Potsie Weber played by actor Anson Williams and Ralph Malph played by Donny Most were his closest friends on the show.

Fonzie actually started off with minimal storylines but as he became more popular with viewers he was given more and more lines in the show. Henry Winkler eventually received top billing with Ron Howard. Once Ron Howard left the show Fonzie became the main character in the show and Winkler received sole top billing. As the show progressed numerous other characters were added or changed.

His character was to wear a black leather jacket but censors made him switch to a white one because they felt the black leather jacket made him look like a hoodlum or thug. He was eventually allowed to wear the black leather jacket on a regular basis. While based on a cool guy look Fonzie was anything but a hoodlum.

He had a high moral code and was always seen sticking up for those who can't defend themselves. He worked as a mechanic and eventually went to night school and got his diploma. In the final season he even adopted an orphaned boy.

There was a popular 1950's nostalgia going on in the 70's and the creators of "Happy Days" tried to cash in on it. The pilot for the show which was originally called "New Family in Town" was rejected in 1971. It was then made into a segment of the television show "Love American Style" as "Love and the Happy Days." In 1972 George Lucas asked to see the pilot to see if Ron Howard could be used in his upcoming movie "American Graffiti." After this the creator of the show Garry Marshall decided to recast the pilot and called it "Happy Days." The new show would premier in January of 1974 and become an American classic. Filming locations for the show are scarce.

The two main sets were the Cunningham home and Arnolds Drive In. The restaurant that was the inspiration for Arnolds was the Milky Way Drive-In located in Glendale, Wisconsin. From my understanding this place is no longer there. The exterior shots of the restaurant on the show are only a set which has since been demolished.

The Cunningham home is real as far as the exterior shots go. The interior was (of course) on a sound stage. The address given in the show is nearly the truth.

On the show the address was 565 N. Clinton Drive in Milwaukee. The real house is at 565 N. Cahuenga Blvd. in Hollywood. The house is nearly identical to how it looked in opening sequences of the show.

In reality it is a six bedroom, two bathroom, and two story house. As far as I can tell there is no apartment above the garage for the Fonze to live in. **This is a private residence so please respect their privacy and do not trespass.**

This house feels so right it can't be wrong, rockin' and rollin' all week long.

***The Historic Pantages Theatre** located at 6233 Hollywood Boulevard. Opened in 1930 this was the home of the Academy Awards for 10 years.*

"The Fresh Prince of Bel-Air"

1990-1996

Our next show is a more modern one (at least as far as my age group is concerned). The show centers on Will Smith who plays a character using his real name. He is a street smart kid from West Philadelphia who gets sent by his mom to live with his aunt and uncle in Bel-Air, California after getting into a fight on the basketball court.

His Uncle Philip is a successful and wealthy judge (played by the late James Avery). His Aunt Vivian was played by Janet Hubert-Whitten in the first 3 seasons and by Daphne Maxwell Reid in the final 3 seasons. The change came about for two reasons. The first being that Will Smith and Janet Hubert-Whitten had some trouble working together and the second being that she became pregnant which was a violation of her contract. They did write it into the script which brought about the character of Nicky played by Ross Bagley.

Other characters were Will's cousins: Carlton (played by Alfonso Ribeiro), Hillary (played by Karyn Parsons), and Ashley (played by Tatyana M. Ali). The butler for the Bank's family was Geoffrey (played by Joseph Marcell). There were others with roles on and off throughout the show but these were the regulars.

The show actually came about in an odd way. According to a “60 Minutes” interview and “Inside the Actors' Studio” Will Smith (who was a rapper in the 1980's) had poor spending habits and underpaid his taxes. The IRS penalized him over 2 million dollars. Much of his property was seized and his wages garnished. He nearly went bankrupt but was approached by NBC who decided to focus a show on him.

There were several locations that the show focused on, such as the student store of the college and Bel-Air Academy. The main focus of the show was on the mansion that the Bank's family lives in. The interior shots were focused on the living room and kitchen primarily.

The kitchen set originally was not attached to the rest of the set. After the first season the living room and kitchen sets were rebuilt larger and attached by an archway. A dining room is occasionally seen as well.

There is a pool house seen in Season 3 but was greatly altered by Season 4 when the boys move into it. A running joke on the show is in regards to Will's friend Jazz. He is often seen being thrown out of the front door of the mansion.

In spite of all the changes with the set the exterior shots of the mansion are the same throughout the show. The only problem is if you want to see the house you better not waste your time in Bel-Air because the actual house used is in the Brentwood area of Los Angeles. As you will see, it is behind a large wall and bushes and is very hard to photograph.

Take my word on it though, having been there twice, it is well worth the visit if you were at all a fan of the show. The house is located at 251 N Bristol Ave. **This is a private residence so please respect their privacy and do not trespass.**

In the picture below you can see the columns on the outside porch of the house.

In the picture below you can see the front of the house a little beyond the driveway.

In the picture below you can get another view of the columns near the front door of the house.

This is his kingdom, I'm finally here where he sat on his throne the prince of Bel-Air!

A great Hollywood landmark is the forecourt at ***Grauman's Chinese Theatre.*** *In the picture above is the signature and prints of Betty Grable whose legs captivated World War 2 era America.*

"Laverne & Shirley"

1976-1983

Laverne & Shirley has always been a favorite of mine. It was one of several spin offs of "Happy Days." They appeared as friends of Fonzie. Other spin offs were "Mork & Mindy," "Joanie Loves Chachi," and the animated show "The Fonze and the Happy Days Gang." Two other shows are in dispute as some claim them to be spin offs and others don't. These are "Blansky's Beauties," and "Out of the Blue."

This show follows the same pattern. It was filmed in the 1970's but is set from the late 50's to the early 60's. Like its predecessor it is also set in Milwaukee, Wisconsin. The show centers on two main characters and several supporting characters. The two main ones are Laverne De Fazio played by Penny Marshall, and Shirley Feeney played by Cindy Williams. The two are single ladies who work in the fictional Shotz Brewery as bottle cappers.

The pair are roommates in a basement apartment. They maintain communication with their upstairs friends by yelling up the dumbwaiter instead of using the telephone. The theme song has always been my favorite part of the show and although the opening sequences changed, the song remained the same.

In seasons 1-6 the show was always the same. It would begin with the two arm in arm, skipping down the street and reciting a Yiddish-American hopscotch chant:

"1, 2, 3, 4, 5, 6, 7, 8, Schlemiel! Schlimazel! Hasenpfeffer Incorporated."

Then they would start the theme song "Making Our Dreams Come True." In seasons 6-7 the show which was previously set in Milwaukee moved to southern California. The opening for those seasons showed Laverne & Shirley coming out of an apartment but still doing their chant before the song starts. In the 8th and final season Shirley had left the show and it shows Laverne watching school kids do the chant before the song begins.

The show was set in Milwaukee for the first six seasons. After that the storyline is that their jobs are replaced by an automated bottling system and they refuse to take jobs as truck washers for the Brewery. They decide to move to Burbank in Southern California to start over.

The story is that their friends and family decide to join them. In the last season actress Cindy Williams became pregnant. When the studio would not meet her demands she left the show. According to storyline her character married a military man and found out she was expecting. Her absence is explained by a note for Laverne that said she went to be with her husband.

I have yet to visit Milwaukee for any filming locations from the first six seasons of the show but I have been to a southern California location. The apartment that the girls moved to in season 7 is located at 419 North Sierra Bonita Avenue in Los Angeles. This is in the Fairfax District. It is located between Melrose Ave. and Beverly Blvd. If you're coming from Hollywood Blvd. take a left onto N. Fairfax Ave. to Santa Monica Blvd. Then hang a left onto Santa Monica. Make a right onto Sierra Bonita Ave.

In the picture you can see there are two apartments side by side so on the outside of the building it will say 419 on one side and 421 on the other. That is the building used in the show. The building still looks the same as it did on the show with the exception of some trees that block a good view of the building from the street but if you stand on the sidewalk you can get good pictures. **This is a private residence so please respect their privacy and do not trespass.**

Time to make all our dreams come true!

419
421

G

The stars on the ***Hollywood Walk of Fame*** *are a must see. This is my favorite actor and comedian.*

"Step By Step"

1991-1998

Step by Step was one of my favorite shows during my high school years. I remember sitting down with a high school girlfriend and watching it before catching the bus to school. I probably watched every episode when they first came out.

The network had the idea to take adults who were popular in the 1970's and make them parents to attract adult viewers. Patrick Duffy was well known for his work on Dallas and in fact the choice in offering him this role was to fulfill their contract to him. They included as his wife Suzanne Somers who was well known for her work on "Three's Company."

Even the child actors they picked were known for appearing on such popular shows as "Baywatch" and "My Two Dads." They hoped by bringing on well-known teens they would attract a solid teen base as well. The series aired on ABC from 1991 to 1997, and CBS from 1997 to 1998.

The show went through several cast changes over the years. One change was adding the character of Cody who was a nephew to Duffy's character Frank Lambert. Cody lived in his van in the family's driveway. He left in 1996.

Brendan Lambert began to disappear slowly over the course of the show and was gone altogether in the last season. They still included him in their count of children in that season. They also added a baby named Lily who was born at the end of one season and then aged five years in between seasons.

The show is based on Frank Lambert, a contractor who is divorced and who has three children: two boys and a girl. While on vacation he meets and marries a widow named Carol Foster, who also has three children: two girls and a boy. They form a family who struggles with resentment, fights, the appearance of favoritism and all that comes in making one family out of two.

The show is set in Port Washington, Wisconsin. The city is a suburb of Milwaukee. The show was filmed at the Warner Bros. Studios in Burbank, but there are several filming locations used for the show outside of the studio.

In the picture below you can see the Six Flags Magic Mountain theme park in Valencia, California. This is where they filmed the opening credits.

In the opening sequence there is a fake ocean with waves breaking right in front of the theme park. The picture below is taken facing where the ocean should be but beyond the fence is just the traffic of Interstate 5.

In the picture on the next page you can see the house that stood in for the Lambert house in the opening sequences and establishing shots of the show. The house is not located in Wisconsin but is actually located near other famous filming locations in southern California.

This was one house that I was super excited to visit in person. It was such a huge part of my growing up years. The address is 2011 Fletcher Avenue in South Pasadena. **This is a private residence so please respect their privacy and do not trespass.**

TV
G

In the picture on the next page you can see the street that the Lambert vehicle is seen passing by in the opening credits. They pass the population sign for Port Washington but the street is actually in southern California not far from the house. The tall building they pass is the South Pasadena Historical Museum and the South Pasadena Preservation Foundation.

The building just beyond the tall building that is labeled "Antiques" in the show is still there but a tree obstructs the view seen in the show. The tall building is actually quite historical. It goes back to 1887 when it was a grocery store, followed by a hotel, then it became a blacksmith shop.

It was here they got a fresh start over and a different hand to play!

IRON WORKS
MUSEUM

*The famous **Hollywood and Vine** intersection gets its fame from its connection to the golden age of Hollywood. These were the first two streets in the new community of Hollywood.*

"Mama's Family"

1974-1978
1983-1984
1986-1990

I have tremendously fond memories of sitting at my Grandma's house and watching shows like Mama's Family. In fact it was my early exposure to comedies like this that forever embedded in my heart a love for these classic shows. This show has always been one of my favorites especially the kitchen set, since I am a fan of yellow kitchens which was a staple of the 1980's.

This show actually appeared three different times. Each time it had a slightly different cast, or format. I want to give a brief overview of the show then look at each appearance of the Harper clan on television.

The show follows the life of the Harper family and most notably the elderly widow Thelma Harper. Her husband Carl had passed away. Thelma is constantly annoyed by her family but deep down she is devoted to them.

In the earlier season she lives with her sister Fran who worked for the local paper. There are appearances by her daughter Ellen who is snobbish and rude, and her daughter Eunice who is whiny and (shall we say) trailer trash.

The early episodes show her taking in her son Vinton and his two children Buzz and Sonja. Vint forms a relationship with Thelma's floozy neighbor Naomi. In later episodes Thelma has a close friendship with her much younger neighbor Iola and we see her nephew Bubba move in.

The family lives in Raytown somewhere in the Midwest. The state is never mentioned in the show but it was possibly based on Raytown, Missouri which is a suburb of Kansas City. The show opens with a song written by Vicki Lawrence who stars as Thelma Harper but the opening of the show has no lyrics and is instrumental only.

Each episode begins by showing Thelma walking out of her house to get the paper. The cast is shown through a series of picture frames in the house. At the end of each episode it was known to cut to an outside shot of the house with Thelma's voice making a jab at whatever was spoken by the last person to talk in that episode.

The first run of the show was as a series of skits on "The Carol Burnett Show" known as "The Family." Unlike the series run, the skits centered on Eunice and Ed and their fights as a couple. In the skit they have two sons but in the series Bubba is listed as an only child.

The skits were so successful they continued until the end of the shows run. They became a made for TV movie in 1982 called "Eunice." The popularity of the movie led to the first incarnation of the television series "Mama's Family."

The show began in 1983 and centered on the Thelma Harper character from "The Family." Thelma played by Vicki Lawrence is widowed and lives with her uptight sister Fran played by Rue McClanahan. Thelma's son Vinton tells her that his wife Mitzi has left the family to be a cocktail waitress in Las Vegas.

He needs a place to live with his two teenage children; Buzz played by Eric Brown, and Sonja played by Karin Argoud. Fran opposes the idea but Thelma takes them in anyways. This leads to many storylines of conflict with Fran.

Vinton forms a friendship with the floozy neighbor Naomi

Oates played by Dorothy Lyman and ends up marrying her. She sells her family home but loses the money in a bad business deal and they have to move into Thelma's basement. In the first season you see Thelma's snobby daughter Ellen (played by Betty White). Another character you see is her spoiled and whiny daughter Eunice played by Carol Burnett. Harvey Korman reprises his role as Ed Higgins as well.

The show was not a big success but it was successful enough to be brought back for a second season. It was canceled halfway through the second season. The network claimed that ratings were too low. The show was revived in 1986 and the last run ended in 1990. Only the characters of Thelma, Naomi, and Vinton were brought back.

Ellen was seen in one episode but was not able to return as a regular because Betty White was already working on "The Golden Girls" and was not available. Fran could not come back because Rue McClanahan was likewise busy with "The Golden Girls." Her character of Fran was killed out in the first episode having choked to death on a toothpick at a bar called the Bigger Jigger.

Eunice and Ed did not return either. They were said to have moved to Florida. Vinton's children Buzz and Sonja are not brought back and except for a brief mention in the first episode are never spoken of again.

In place of them they brought in Bubba Higgins played by Allan Kayser. Bubba is the son of Eunice and Ed who was mentioned in the Carol Burnett skits but never seen. He is ordered to live with Thelma after being released from Juvenile Hall on probation.

Another new character was the neighbor Iola Boylan played by Beverly Archer. She is Thelma's best friend but is around Vinton's age. She has a crush on Vint that he always seems oblivious to. She was known for saying, "knock, knock" as she walked in the house instead of ringing the doorbell or actually knocking. The show ended in 1990 with Naomi giving birth to a baby girl named Tiffany Thelma.

The house seen in the opening and closing of the show is not located in Raytown nor is it in the Midwest. It is actually located near other filming locations on a quaint street in South Pasadena, California. The house pictured on the next page is how it looked in 2012.

The color of the house has changed from a white and yellow to a white and green. The only real difference is the white picket enclosed area of the porch is gone now. Other than that, the house is identical to how it looked in the show. The address is 1027 Montrose Avenue in South Pasadena. **This is a private residence so please respect their privacy and do not trespass.**

This has been the "Mama's Family" house or my name isn't Thelma Harper!

"Benson"

1979-1986

One of my favorite shows as a kid was "Benson." For some reason that show really sticks out in my head. I mostly watched reruns as a kid and have not watched it much since reaching adulthood.

The show is a spinoff of the soap opera parody "Soap." In that show the character of Benson had worked as a butler for the Tate family. I never watched that show so all I know of the character is what I saw on this one.

In "Benson" the title character Benson DuBois is played by Robert Guillaume. Benson was hired by the widowed Governor to be head of household affairs for him and his daughter. The Governor's character is a cousin to the family on "Soap." The state in which this show took place was never named although "Soap" took place in Connecticut.

The show was centered mainly on Benson's housekeeping dilemmas. It documented his ongoing fights with the German cook named Gretchen. It also involved his dealings with John Taylor who assisted Governor Gatling as chief of staff.

Jerry Seinfeld played a minor part during 3 episodes in 1980. He played a small role as Frankie, a delivery boy and unsuccessful comedian. He left the show due to creative differences.

During the show Benson worked his way up the ladder. He moved from the Head of Household Affairs to State Budget Director. It was at this point that his last name was revealed to the audience.

He eventually was promoted to the position of Lieutenant Governor. Benson actually ran against Gatling for the office of Governor in the final episodes of the 1985–1986 season. The German cook who by this time had moved up to head of household affairs became Benson's biggest supporter. He ended up making her his personal assistant and campaign manager.

The show had a memorable ending. It was centered originally on the premise that Gatling was prohibited from running for re-election due to term limits. It was later revealed that he could run again as an independent candidate.

He decided to run again. Benson by this time had already won the nomination of the party. This set the stage for the two to run against each other in the general election.

Election night was shown on the final episode and the race was too close to call. Benson and Gatling, who had strained relations because of the race, made peace and sat down to watch election returns together. The announcement came that a winner in the close election was being projected.

The episode ended with a freeze frame of Benson and Gatling, just as the announcement began. This left the series with a cliffhanger. In 2007 it was said that if the show had continued Gatling would have won and Benson would have become a senator.

The mansion shown in the opening sequences of the show was not located in a big gated community. In fact I was surprised by how open the property was when I arrived. The house is located at 1365 South Oakland Avenue in Pasadena. **This is a private residence so please respect their privacy and do not trespass.**

This has been the Benson house... I can hear you!

"I Love Lucy"

1951-1960

This is one show that nearly all people are familiar with. It starred Lucille Ball, Desi Arnaz, William Frawley, and Vivian Vance, not to mention a multitude of guest stars. Actors such as Frank Nelson, John Wayne, Harpo Marx, Bill Holden, Gale Gordon, and Rock Hudson all made appearances on Lucy. George Reeves appeared as his "Superman" character as well.

The series originally ran in black and white from October 1951 through May 1957. It ran on the CBS network. The episodes were done in a half hour format.

From 1957 to 1960 the show continued under the name of "The Lucille Ball-Desi Arnaz Show." This show kept the same characters and setting but changed to an hour long format. In reruns they aired as "The Lucy-Desi Comedy Hour."

This show was the first scripted show to be filmed in front of a live studio audience and to be shot on 35mm film. "I Love Lucy" was the most watched television show in the United States during its first four seasons. When they went off the air they were the first show to do so at the top of the ratings. "The Andy Griffith Show" and "Seinfeld" would later achieve this feat.

The show was set on the New York City apartment of a couple named Ricky and Lucy Ricardo. Other main players are the landlords Fred and Ethel Mertz as well as neighbor Mrs. Trumbull, and Lucy's mother Mrs. McGillicuddy. In Season 2 the Ricardos have a baby named Ricky Ricardo Jr. who goes by the name Little Ricky.

Lucy can best be described as naïve and zealous to be in show business much to the chagrin of Ricky. She often enlists the help of Fred and Ethel in attempts to get into the show. Fred and Ethel are former Vaudevillians (and unlike Lucy) actually have talent, which leads Ricky to often put them to work in his show.

Lucy and Ricky Ricardo as legendary as they are almost never existed. Under the original premise of the show they were to be called Lucy and Larry Lopez.

In the picture on the next page you can see the hotel that was used in Season 4, Episode 13. This episode was called “Hollywood at Last.” The hotel is seen as the group pull into the hotel on arrival.

The hotel is called the Beverly Palms Hotel in the show but is actually named The Avalon Hotel. At the time of the show it was a residential motel called the Beverly Carlton. Marilyn Monroe lived here in room 305 of the Beverly building. The hotel is made up of three buildings. The other two are the Canon and the Olympic.

The hotel is located at 9400 West Olympic Boulevard in Beverly Hills. It looks remarkably much like it did in the 1950's.

SPEED
LIMIT
25

During the same season while the Ricardos and Mertzes are in Hollywood, Lucy and Ethel take a bus tour. This tour takes them to see some of the homes of the movie stars. The episode is called "The Tour."

While on this tour Lucy drags Ethel off the bus to pick a grapefruit form the home of Richard Widmark. The bus leaves once they get off of it, stranding them at the house. Lucy climbs the wall but falls into his backyard.

Finding herself unable to climb back over the wall and with a guard dog after her Lucy goes into the house to try and escape. The phone rings and Lucy tries to avoid being caught by the housekeeper by hiding. When Richard Widmark comes home with Ricky in tow, Lucy hides under a bear rug. Comedy ensues as a large dog comes in to lay on Lucy.

In this episode the house that stands in for Richard Widmark's is actually the home of Lucy and Desi Arnaz. They get off the bus on the corner of Lexington and Roxbury as pictured on the next page. Lucy's house looks different because it was torn down and rebuilt but is located at 1000 North Roxbury in Beverly Hills. **This is a private residence so please respect their privacy and do not trespass.**

In the picture below you can see the studio where Seasons 3-6 were filmed. Back then it was called Desilu and by the time shows like "The Golden Girls" were filmed it was called RenMar Studios. Today it's called Red Studios. The studio is located at 846 N. Cahuenga Blvd. in Hollywood.

The next page shows the background you see from the Ricardos balcony in the Hollywood episodes. The view is of the Hollywood and Vine intersection. My picture was taken from the Selma and Vine intersection.

Much has changed. The famous Capitol Records building is there now. It wasn't seen in the show because it was still being built at the time.

The Broadway building is still there as well as the Taft building. You can see the sign for The Broadway in the show as well as the advertisement on the Taft building.

On the second page you can see the little booth outside of the Grauman's Chinese Theatre in Hollywood. The booth can be seen in the "I Love Lucy" episode where Lucy steals John Wayne's footprints.

No she can't be in the show!

JET LAG.
1600 VINE

INFORMATION
STARLINE TOURS
STARLINE TOURS

Actress Norma Talmadge was the first to leave her prints in the forecourt of ***Grauman's Chinese Theater****. Located at 6925 Hollywood Blvd. little could she have known the tradition she was starting! History may have forgotten her, but she will always be the first in wet cement.*

"Three's Company"

1977-1984

This show has one of my favorite theme songs of all. Of course I say that about nearly every 80's show but this truly is one of the best. This is one show I watch even today when I get the chance.

It aired between March of 1977 and September of 1984. This means I was 3 years old when the show went off the air. Needless to say my history with it comes from reruns.

The show is actually based on a British comedy called "Man About the House." For the American version of it, the show centers on three single roommates. Janet, Chrissy, and Jack all live together (platonically) in an apartment in Santa Monica. Their landlords are Stanley and Helen Roper.

A few cast changes took place over the course of the show. Suzanne Somers (who played Chrissy Snow) left the show and was replaced first by Jenilee Harrison who played Cindy Snow which was supposed to be Chrissy's cousin. When Jenilee left the show she was replaced by Priscilla Barnes who played Terri Alden.

The Ropers left to star in their own show. The spin-off was called "The Ropers" and aired for only one season between 1979 and 1980. They were replaced by Don Knotts who played the trio's new landlord Ralph Furley.

The show was set in Santa Monica, but I never thought I would find the actual exterior used for the show in that city. Most of the time even when a show is set in Los Angeles the exterior shots are taken in a different city than the show describes. This show was the exception.

It's not an easy house to find. The house is well hidden behind green vines and trees. It is actually a house and not an apartment complex as it is portrayed on television. It does have the look of an apartment which is what made it perfect for use on the show.

As you can see in the picture on the next page the building is remarkably the same as it appeared on the show. The only real difference today is the missing round brown door. Other than that it looks the same as it did before.

The “Three's Company” house (apartment) is located at 2912 4th Street in Santa Monica. **This is a private residence so please respect their privacy and do not trespass.**

Whatever you do, don't come and knock on their door!

“Party of Five”

1994-2000

I watched this show off and on during my teenage years. "Party of Five" was actually set to be cancelled after having low ratings. It became one of the lowest rated shows to win the Golden Globe for best drama.

The show launched the career of several stars. It produced a spin-off called "Time of Your Life" which lasted for only one season. The show centers on the Salinger family who were orphaned when their parents were killed by a drunk driver. The show is set in San Francisco. Much of the storyline centers on the struggles of the siblings trying to make their way and deal with life's issues.

In the picture on the next page you can see the house used to establish the exterior shots for the show. The house remains exactly the same as it was on the show and is a beautiful home to look at. It is located at 2311 Broadway in the Pacific Heights neighborhood of San Francisco. **This is a private residence so please respect their privacy and do not trespass.**

Remember everyone wants to be closer to free!

*The **Historic Hollywood First National Bank Building** located at 6777 Hollywood Blvd.*

"Ozzie and Harriet"

1952-1966

This classic television show was centered on a real life family known as the Nelsons. Ozzie, Harriet and their sons David and Ricky. This was the first television show to make the 10 year mark in terms of run time.

In the 1930's Ozzie Nelsons orchestra was booked at the Glen Island Casino which brought national attention to him. In 1933 Ozzie and Harriet worked on “The Baker's Broadcast.” During the run of this radio show they were married.

They decided to stay in radio in order to work together and in 1941 joined the cast of “The Red Skelton Show.” The Nelsons stayed with this show until Red was drafted in 1944. After this Ozzie formed his own situation comedy based on his family called “The Adventures of Ozzie and Harriet.”

Ozzie wanted to know if his family would be as popular on screen as they were on radio. In 1952 they starred with Rock Hudson in a film called “Here Come the Nelsons.” The reaction assured Ozzie that the transition could be made. They continued their radio show while working on the television show.

Ozzie Nelson made a unique contract for the television show which guaranteed payment whether or not the show was cancelled. The show made every attempt to be real. The house used for the exterior shots was the actual house that the Nelsons lived in. The sets for the interior shots were designed to look like their actual house.

Storylines were often based on true life situations. When the boys married, their wives joined the cast and the marriages were written into the script. One fact not written into the show was Ozzie's career. An ongoing joke was that Ozzie never left the house except to get ice cream.

By the middle of the 1960's it became clear that America's social climate was changing. Ozzie tried to make the show relevant but viewers never picked up on it. They even transitioned to color. The show ran for a total of 14 seasons and is a part of American television history.

The pictures on the next page are of the Ozzie and Harriet house located at 1822 Camino Palmero Street in Hollywood off of Franklin Avenue, not far from Hollywood Boulevard. **This is a private residence so please respect their privacy and do not trespass.**

This has been the show starring the entire Nelson family.

“Just the Ten of Us”

1988-1990

This show was a spin-off of the popular comedy "Growing Pains." The pilot episode was on "Growing Pains" before moving to its own slot on the schedule. The focus of the show is a Catholic gym teacher named Graham Lubbock.

He was a teacher at the high school that "Growing Pains" parents Mike and Carol Seaver attended. Graham is the father of 8 children. In the pilot we learn that Graham's job is in danger due to budget cuts. Mike Seaver leads a protest after finding out that Graham is supporting a large family.

Graham loses his job but gets another one at St. Augustine's School in Eureka, California. Even though the school is an all-boys school Lubbock has 6 girls which are allowed to attend much to the joy of the male student body. The show deals with common family issues such as money and dating.

The house pictured on the next page was used for the opening sequences and is located at 15548 Iron Canyon Road in Canyon Country. **This is a private residence so please respect their privacy and do not trespass.**

This has been the "Just the Ten of Us" house where they were doing it the best they could!

just
THE TEN of US

*This is the **Hollywood History Museum** at 1660 N. Highland. This building is the former Max Factor Studio where many stars were clients during the golden age of Hollywood. This is where Lucille Ball became a redhead.*

"The Hogan Family"

1986-1991

This show was originally called “Valerie.” It starred Valerie Harper as a mom struggling to raise her three sons. Her airline pilot husband is gone for long periods of time.

Valerie Harper was on the show for two seasons before deciding to demand more money. During a break in filming she said that she would not return unless her demands were met. An agreement was reached and Harper returned to film.

After the first episode was finished she began to hold out again with more demands. The show filmed around her for a few episodes until after not showing up for filming of three episodes in a row Harper was written out. The storyline was that her character had been killed in a car accident.

She was replaced by Sandy Duncan who moved in as the aunt to take care of the children. The name of the show was changed to “Valerie's Family: The Hogans.” Eventually the name of the show became simply known as “The Hogan Family.”

On the next page is the house that was used for exterior shots during the show. The house looks just as it did during filming of the show. I got chills standing in front of the house, it was so much like what I had seen on television.

If you ever watched this show then standing in front of this house makes you feel as if you're on the show yourself. The address is 840 Bellefontaine Place in Pasadena. **This is a private residence so please respect their privacy and do not trespass.**

This has been “The Hogan Family” house and as they say Life is such a sweet insanity.

Part 2:

Movie Filming Locations

"Larry Crowne"

2011

“Larry Crowne” is truly a movie I watched by accident. I was at my sister's house and I was working on another project and swore I had no interest in the new Tom Hanks movie. I looked up every few minutes to relax and pretty soon found myself watching the entire movie with my project unfinished. At the end I had to go back and watch the beginning to put pieces together.

The title character Larry is played by Tom Hanks who is one of my favorite living actors. He plays a Navy veteran who has reached middle age and is suddenly fired from his job at a retail store due to his lack of a college education.

Larry is unable to find work and finds himself in danger of losing his home. He is divorced and lives alone although his neighbor Lamar (played by Cedric the Entertainer) plays a big role in the movie. Lamar suggests that he enroll in the community college.

Unable to afford his SUV, Larry buys a scooter to get around. While in college he takes a speech class taught by Julia Roberts and economics taught by George Takei. He gains a job from his friend Frank who runs a diner.

Julia Roberts' character drinks at home due to her unhappy marriage to Dean. He was a professor but turned to internet blogging. This was in large part a cover for his long hours spent watching internet pornography.

Larry's friend Talia invites him to join a scooter club. This club is led by her boyfriend (played by Wilmer Valderrama). This scooter club plays an important role in the movie.

Larry and his scooter club come across Julia Roberts at a bus stop after she had a bad fight with her husband. Larry offers her a ride home and she accepts. While on their way they see her husband Dean getting arrested for drunk driving.

At her front door they kiss but Larry refuses to take it further not wanting to take advantage of her since she was intoxicated. When Dean gets home the next morning he finds all of his belongings on the front lawn. Larry uses what he has learned in economics class to start a strategic foreclosure since he realizes he will lose his house.

Talia announces she is dropping out of college to open a thrift store and Mercedes finally learns that Larry and Talia are just friends. Mercedes divorces Dean. When finals come Larry gives a speech that draws a round of applause not only from his classmates but from Mercedes who is now much more fulfilled in her career and life.

Mercedes shows up at Larry's diner and tells him that she gave him an A+. She lets him know that he was an excellent student and he lets her know that she was an excellent teacher. When the next semester arrives Larry doesn't register for her class but instead registers for a second term economics class.

When Mercedes arrives back in her office she sees a note from Larry inviting her to dinner and it contains the address to his new apartment. She arrives at his new place and the movie ends with them going in and closing the door.

On the next page is the picture of the “Larry Crowne” house. It looks amazingly as it did in the movie just a few years ago. The house is located at the end of a cul-de-sac and the actual address numbers are used in the movie.

The house is located at 8656 Balcom Avenue in Northridge. **This is a private residence so please respect their privacy and do not trespass.**

8656

8656

In the movie Larry's neighbor Lamar always seemed to have a yard sale going on. The house appears in the movie to be at the end of the cul-de-sac like Larry's house. In reality it is on the same street but it's on the side of the street not at the end.

This house also looks amazingly the same as it did on the show with very little (if any) changes to it. The picture on the next page is of Lamar's house which is located at 8642 Balcom Avenue in Northridge. **This is a private residence so please respect their privacy and do not trespass.**

In the movie Larry gets a job at a diner thanks to his friend Frank. This job helps him make ends meet while in college. This diner serves as a major background for many scenes in the movie.

When I first saw the movie I thought perhaps it was located on a studio lot. You can imagine my surprise and joy when I realized it was an actual diner that was open for business. I set out to find this location at once.

I found out that it was Frank's Restaurant at 916 West Olive Avenue in Burbank. I totally recommend stopping by Frank's if you're in the area. It looks exactly as it did in the movie and it's only a mile or two from other Burbank filming locations.

The picture on the next page is from my first visit to Frank's but believe me there have been others.

FRANK'S RESTAURANT

FRANKS
COFFEE SHOP
STEAKS
RANK'S RESTAURANT

On the next few pages are pictures of Mercedes' apartment building in the movie. The first one is the exterior of the apartment building which looks exactly as it did in the movie. It is located at 325 South Orange Grove Blvd. in Pasadena.

The entrance seen in the movie does not face Orange Grove. This can make it hard to find. It is actually located on the side street of Arbor.

The second page shows a tree in front of the complex which can clearly be seen in the movie. The third page shows the front door to Mercedes' and Dean's apartment. The apartment number is 325. **Please respect the privacy of the residents and do not trespass.**

The next “Larry Crowne” location is both the storefront of Talia's store as well as Larry's apartment from the closing scenes of the movie. The building looks so simple that it's easy to pass by it without a second glance.

The front of the building was used for the store and the apartment is located upstairs in the same building. On the next page is the front of the building. If you look closely at the screenshot you can see the building as it appears today.

The rounded front facing the corner as well as the big window give it away. You have to know what you're looking for to find this one. I totally recommend visiting this location if you're in the area as well as watching the movie if you haven't yet. The second page shows a building across the street that is visible in a shot where all the scooters are parked outside the building. That building is actually a school but I recognized it immediately.

The third and fourth pages show Larry's apartment (or at least as much of it as we can see). The gate leading to the stairs is locked so we could only take pictures from the sidewalk. The “Larry Crowne” apartment building is located at 906 Boston Street and the storefront is at 2104 North Lake Avenue in Altadena.

Rick Garland

"The Mask"

1994

Of my favorite movies during my teenage years "The Mask" was a regular for me. I had already come to love Jim Carrey from "Ace Ventura: Pet Detective." His brand of slapstick, physical comedy was what drew me to his movies. As a lover of comedies I took in every second of Jim Carrey's antics with enthusiasm. He is still one of my favorite modern comedic actors.

Jim Carrey plays Stanley Ipkiss. Stanley is a shy bank clerk who is always pushed around by everyone. His co-worker Charlie and his Jack Russell Terrier named Milo are truly his best friends.

Gangster Dorian Tyrell who runs a nightclub called the Coco Bongo sends his girlfriend Tina into Stanley's bank. Her job was to record the layout so they could plan a robbery. Stanley is attracted to Tina who seems attracted to him as well.

Stanley attempts to go into the Coco Bongo but is denied entrance. Stanley goes to the city harbor where he finds a wooden mask. When he puts on the mask it's shown to have special powers. It turns him into a bizarre and green faced wild man.

He finds himself able to alter himself and his surroundings in a cartoonish way. He uses these abilities to get revenge on those who have tormented him. One of those being his auto mechanic who ripped him off. He finds himself attacked by a street gang only to win by turning himself into a tommy gun.

He finds out the mask is an image of Loki the Norse god of darkness and mischief. While wearing the mask Stanley raids the bank and convinces the police force trying to catch him to join him in a giant performance of the Desi Arnaz song "Cuban Pete."

The movie ends with Stanley and Tina getting together, the bad guys being caught, and the mask being thrown back into the harbor only to be retrieved by Milo.

The picture on the next page is the mechanic's shop that Stanley goes to in the movie. The building is actually an old firehouse which was also used for interior shots in Ghostbusters.

The scenes were filmed at Fire Station #23 in Downtown Los Angeles. The address is 225 East 5th Street.

ENGINE 23 TRUCK CO.

SHOCK
ABSORBERS
TIRES

"Return of the Living Dead"

1985

This movie chronicles the events surrounding the accidental release of hungry zombies. They are battled by three men and a group of punk teenagers. In previous zombie movies such as “Night of the Living Dead” zombies only ate flesh but this movie introduced the idea of zombie's craving brains.

In the movie they capture a zombie and tie her to a table. They ask her why she wants brains. It is revealed that zombies can feel themselves dying and eating brains makes the pain go away.

This movie was a success at the box office and led to four sequels by the same name. The movie is full of 80's death metal and punk music. I believe this is also the first movie where zombies are able to run and fight as opposed to being slow moving hordes.

The movie is set in a medical supply warehouse in Louisville, Kentucky. The building used for the exterior shots is actually a building just off Interstate 5 in Downtown Los Angeles. The address is 698 Moulton Avenue. **This is a private property so please do not trespass.**

*This is the location of the old **Hollywood Brown Derby**. The building was torn down and rebuilt but the lower half retains the same architecture. This was where Clark Gable proposed to Carol Lombard. It is located behind the Taft Building at Hollywood and Vine.*

"Buffy the Vampire Slayer"

1992

This movie (which is not as well-known as the television series which followed) was one of my favorites growing up. The main character Buffy (played by Kristy Swanson), is a stereotypical cheerleader consumed only with shopping, her friends, and boyfriend. The movie is set in Los Angeles.

One day at school Buffy is approached by a man named Merrick Jamison-Smythe (played by Donald Sutherland). He claims that she is the slayer or chosen one and that he is a watcher who is responsible to train Buffy. Buffy rejected this claim at first, but later accepted it once Merrick told her of a recurring dream she had been having.

Oliver Pike (played by Luke Perry) and his best friend Benny (played by David Arquette) are resentful of Buffy and her friends. They are out drinking one night when they are suddenly attacked by vampires. Benny becomes a vampire but Oliver escapes with the help of Merrick. Benny visits Oliver in an attempt to get him to join them.

Buffy has some successful battles against vampires leading to her being drawn into battle with a local vampire king called Lothos. He has killed a number of slayers in the past. Buffy, Merrick, and Oliver get into battle with Amilyn (played by Paul Reubins) who is a right hand man of Lothos. Amilyn loses his arm in the battle and retreats to speak with Lothos.

Lothos realizes that Buffy is the slayer. Oliver and Buffy begin a romantic interest at this point. Oliver becomes her partner in fighting vampires.

During a school basketball game Buffy and Oliver find out one of the players works for Lothos. A chase follows leading to a storage yard for parade floats. They defeat the gang of vampires leading to a showdown with Lothos.

He places Buffy in a hypnotic trance. Merrick intervenes to break the trance and is finally impaled and killed. Lothos leaves saying Buffy is not ready.

Merrick's death leads to Buffy forsaking her friends as well as her duties as a slayer. Buffy and Oliver meet at the senior dance and kiss as vampires invade the dance. Buffy goes outside to fight the creatures while Oliver stays inside to fight his former friend Benny.

After defeating the vampires Buffy confronts Lothos and kills Amilyn. Buffy is again hypnotized but breaks it by making a flame thrower out of a cross and hairspray which burns Lothos.

The battle ends with Buffy killing Lothos by impaling him. The movie ends with Oliver and Buffy leaving on a motorcycle. It's not as dark as the author intended but I still think it's a great movie and one I enjoy watching. Luke Perry was huge at the time and it's sad to me that his fame didn't last longer than it did. Kristy Swanson is a great actress and nailed this part with humor and depth.

The only location I have found from this movie is a carousel that we see Amilyn riding on as he is stalking a boy from Buffy's high school before making him a vampire.

The carousel is seen in many movies and is located in Griffith Park in Los Angeles

Rick Garland

*The world famous **Hollywood Wax Museum** at 6767 Hollywood Blvd.*

"Maid to Order"

1987

Much to my surprise this is a little known movie but I recommend to all of my readers to get it immediately and watch it. Growing up this was one I watched often. Even today I love the 1980's. The music, television, cartoons, pro-wrestling and movies of that decade are in my opinion some of the greatest of all time.

The main character is Jessie Montgomery (played by Ally Sheedy) who is a wonderful actress. She plays a rich party girl who has no respect for herself or others. Her selfish lifestyle soon comes crashing down around her.

After being arrested for driving under the influence she pushes her father to his limit. Her father is played by an equally wonderful actor Tom Skerritt. After this event he says the one thing he thought he would never say. He says he wishes he never had a daughter.

After this wish comes Stella played by another wonderful actress Beverly D'Angelo. Stella makes it as though Jessie's life never existed. As far as her father is concerned he never had a daughter and Jessie must learn to survive on her own. She goes to work as a maid for a wealthy eccentric couple known as the Starkey's.

She interacts with the other staff members in the mansion and through these interactions learns the meaning of love, self-respect and friendship. She finally learns to put others before herself and is rewarded with her old life back. This film is a must see if you never have seen it.

The mansion used for the exterior shots of Jessie's father's house is located at 365 South Hudson Avenue in Los Angeles. The house looks pretty much the same is it did in the movie. **This is a private residence so please respect their privacy and do not trespass.**

The house where Jessie served as a maid is located at 32596 Pacific Coast Highway in Malibu but there is really no place to pull over and get a good view of the house. The part of the exterior used is not visible from the street and the house is up on a hill blocked by trees. If you attempt to see it be careful as that is a high traffic area and there is no sidewalk. **This too is a private residence so please respect their privacy and do not trespass.**

The pictures on the next page are of the Hudson mansion which was Jessie's father's house.

"Father of the Bride"

1991

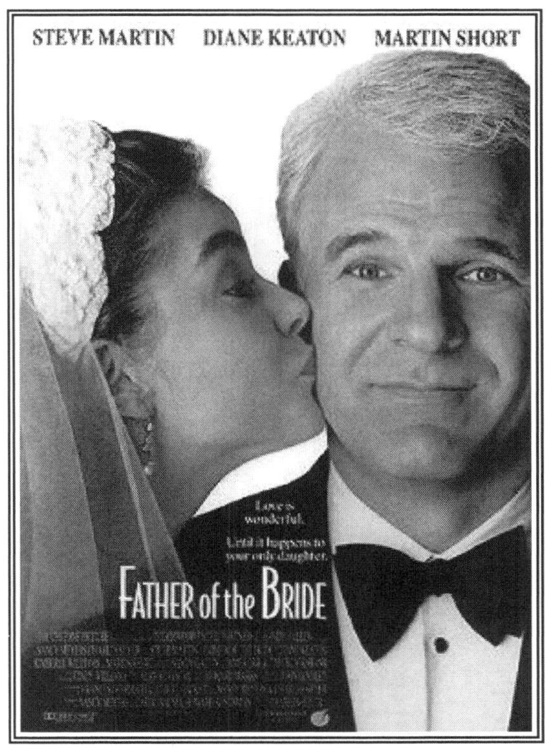

This is perhaps one of the best films Steve Martin ever worked on and one of the most beloved of the 1990's. I have met very few people in my day who have never heard of this movie. If you're one who has never seen it then I urge you put down this book and watch it.

Steve Martin plays George Banks. The movie is set in San Marino, California. Banks owns an athletic shoe company. He has a beautiful house, a loving wife (played by the wonderful Diane Keaton) and two children.

His world seems perfect until his 22 year old daughter Annie comes home from Europe and announces her marriage to Brian MacKenzie. He is from a wealthy family in Bel-Air but the catch is that they have only known each other a few months.

The reunion turns into a heated fight which is reconciled in time for George to meet Brian. He has a good financial situation and a great personality but in spite of all this George hates Brian from the start. His wife Nina loves Brian from the first meeting.

The movie follows the slow but sure breakdown of George Banks. First he meets Brian's parents and their ferocious pet Dobermans. Then he learns the high cost of the wedding at $250 a head. Then there is the eccentric wedding planner played by the living legend Martin Short.

George finally breaks down in a supermarket which leads to his arrest. His wife bails him out only after making him promise to stay out of the wedding preparations. He agrees and does his best.

There are many last minute problems such as a strange winter blast which brings snow to Southern California. Parking proves disastrous which leads to George missing Annie throwing her bouquet. George makes several attempts to see Annie before they leave on their honeymoon but he misses her. Annie calls from the airport to thank him.

The pictures on the next page are of the house used in the movie. As far as I know the inside as well as the backyard were all used in the filming of the movie. The house from the outside looks exactly as it did in the movie. I can't point to one difference. It is located in Pasadena, which is actually near San Marino, California.

The address of the house is 843 South El Molino. **This is a private residence so please respect their privacy and do not trespass.**

The other location I have been to from this movie is the bridal shop. Unfortunately you can't really see the outside that good in the movie and the store was closed the day I was there. If you stop by there when they are open you can see the interior which is still very similar.

It can be a little hard to find but once you do it's very rewarding if you are a fan of the movie as I am. The picture of the building is below. The address is 8408 Melrose Place in West Hollywood.

The Historic Roosevelt Hotel *at 7000 Hollywood Blvd. A must see on any Hollywood trip. It's even rumored that stars such as Marilyn Monroe still haunt the hotel.*

"Rumor Has It"

2005

I happened to pick this movie up one day out of boredom and fell in love with it. I thought the acting and storyline were excellent. If you have not seen it I encourage you to try it out.

Sarah Huttinger (played by the beautiful Jennifer Aniston) travels from New York to Pasadena for her sister's wedding. Her fiancé Jeff Daly played by Mark Ruffalo joins her on the trip. This trip will change their lives.

Sarah learns from her grandmother Katharine (played by Shirley Maclaine) that prior to her parents wedding her mother ran off to Cabo San Lucas to see her classmate Beau Burroughs. Jeff points out that her parents were married just short of nine months before her birth. This brings her to the conclusion that Beau might be her actual father. She learns that her grandmother may have actually been the inspiration for the character of Mrs. Robinson in the novel "The Graduate."

Sarah decides to find Beau. She flies to San Francisco and corners him at a conference. He confesses to the affair but assures her that due to trauma from a high school soccer game he could not be her father because he is sterile. They go out for drinks and the next day Sarah wakes up in his home in Half Moon Bay.

Sarah feels guilty about what happened but still goes with Beau to a charity ball as his date. At the event she meets his son Blake. It's explained by Beau that since he was sterile they had a son through artificial insemination.

Sarah understands and gives Beau a kiss just as Jeff walks in. He came to California to find her. Jeff leaves following an argument. Sarah talks with Katherine who is angry that Beau has been with her granddaughter.

The two women learn that Annie suffered an anxiety attack on her way to her honeymoon. Sarah tells her sister about Beau's relationship with three generations in her family. In the process she realizes she is ready to marry Jeff.

Sarah returns to New York to tell Jeff her feelings. It appears as though he rejects her but in the end he does accept her back. They agree that if they have a daughter she is not to go near Beau. The house from the movie is actually really close to the house from "Father of the Bride." I have them both in here together so that you can see them both at the same time. It is located at 717 South Hudson in Pasadena. **This is a private residence so please respect their privacy and do not trespass.**

If you notice in my picture there is a lamp post by the sidewalk. I have included here a shot from the movie showing the same lamp post.

The other house I have visited from this movie is the house that belonged to Aunt Mitsy in the movie. It is seen only briefly in one scene. Sarah goes to her to find out information about her mother who was dead.

This was where she found out that her family may have been the inspiration for “The Graduate.” There is also a large yellow house seen in the background as the two ladies are talking. I was able to get pictures of both houses which will follow on the next two pages.

The house is actually an apartment building and has an amazingly large and beautiful front porch. If you're in the area to see the one house then come see these as well.

This house is located at 485 Ellis Street in Pasadena. **This is a private residence so please respect their privacy and do not trespass.** The big yellow house seen in the movie is across the street.

"A Nightmare on Elm Street"

1984

This is the first horror movie I ever watched and is without a doubt one of the kings of the slasher film genre. I, like so many others, had trouble going to sleep afraid my dreams would yield death. I'm sure most have watched it but if you haven't then make sure you do.

High School students Tina, Nancy, Glen and Rod are friends who share the same nightmare about being stalked by the same man with a glove of razors. One night they all stay at Tina's house because her parents are out of town. Rod awakens to find Tina going through a nightmare. When the mysterious figure goes in for the kill he can see her being slashed and carried up the wall and across the ceiling. Her screaming and calling Rod's name alerts the others.

Rod is the only one that was in the room with Tina and is suspected of her murder. He is arrested the next day. Nancy has a dream at school the following day and is attacked by the same man who killed Tina. She leaves school early to talk to Rod at the jail.

Rod tells her of the man with the glove who is also in his nightmares as well as Nancy's. At this point Nancy realizes that Rod didn't kill Tina at all. Nancy tells her boyfriend Glen to watch her while she sleeps so that she can investigate her dreams. He reluctantly agrees and while she dreams she sees the killer go into Rod's jail cell.

Upon waking she and Glen go to the jail to find that Rod was found hung by his own sheets. Suicide is presumed by all except for Nancy and Glen. They believe someone was in the cell with him.

During Rod's funeral Nancy's mother decides to get her daughter mental help. Nancy goes to a clinic to evaluate her dreams but has a violent encounter while there. She wakes up with a streak of white in her hair and a slash on her arm. Nancy pulls the killers dirty brown hat out of the dream much to the horror of her mom who recognizes the hat.

Nancy's mother begins to drink heavily and has security bars installed on her home on Elm Street. Here much of the story comes together. She tells Nancy that the hat belongs to the burned man in her nightmares whom she reveals to be Freddy Krueger.

He lived in the neighborhood 20 years earlier and was arrested for murdering 20 children. He was released based on a technicality. After his release the parents burned Freddy alive. It becomes apparent to her mother that Freddy is now getting revenge from beyond the grave by killing the children from their dreams.

Nancy relates to Glen what she learns from her mother.

He urges her to take away the power of Freddy by not being afraid of him. Nancy has other plans.

She plans to pull Freddy out of the dream world so that she and Glen can defeat him. The problem is that both have been confined to their houses by their parents. Glen falls asleep and Freddy pulls him into his bed sending out a fountain of blood.

Nancy goes into her dreams to hunt Freddy and grabs him as her alarm goes off thus bringing him into her world. She ends up setting Freddy on fire and trapping him in the basement before calling her dad. He arrives with other police to put out the fires. Nancy follows a trail of footprints to her mother's room where she finds Freddy smothering her with his body which is on fire.

Freddy disappears and her mother's body vanishes into the bed. Nancy turns her back as Freddy rises from the bed. Nancy declares she is no longer afraid of him. This takes away his power and he vanishes as he jumps for her.

Nancy leaves the room and steps out into the sunlight. Her mom appears sober and promises not to drink anymore. She gets into Glen's convertible with her friends. The convertible top which is the same fabric as Freddy's sweater clamps shut locking her in. Her mother is grabbed by Freddy and pulled through the front door window of the house.

I have been able to find a good number of locations for this movie. On the next page you will see the high school used in the movie. The high school is John Marshall High School at 3939 Tracy Street in Los Angeles not far from Griffith Park.

On the second page you will find Nancy's house (which is the most well-known). It has changed very little except the blue door is now red. This house is located at 1428 North Genessee Avenue in Hollywood. It's pretty much right off Sunset Blvd. **This is a private residence so please respect their privacy and do not trespass.**

On the third page you will see the house which belonged to Nancy's boyfriend Glen (played by Johnny Depp). It is located almost right across the street at 1419 Genessee Avenue. **This is a private residence so please respect their privacy and do not trespass.**

On the next few pages you will see the cemetery used in the movie. The first picture is of a chapel where Nancy is talking to her mother. The second is of a grave visible behind her father when he arrives to talk to her.

The third and fourth picture is of the spot where Rod's grave was placed. The tree is still there as well as the little figure on one of the graves. His gravesite was located behind the real life graves of Louise Minier and Belle Kuster.

The cemetery used is the oldest in Los Angeles and contains the final resting places of many founders of the city. It was filmed at Evergreen Memorial Park and Crematory located at 204 North Evergreen Avenue in Los Angeles.

COULTER
McREYNOLDS

STARK

The picture below is of the building where the boiler room scenes were filmed for the movie. They were filmed in the basement. The building today looks so creepy that I would never venture into the basement to get pictures even if I could.

These scenes were filmed at the Lincoln Heights Jail located at 421 North Avenue 19 in Downtown Los Angeles. Take pictures and enjoy but don't break the law. **This is private property so please do not trespass.**

The building used as the jail is on the next three pages. This building is actually the Los Angeles Library Cahuenga Branch located at 4591 Santa Monica Blvd. The inside looks different (having been remodeled) but the outside is identical to the movie.

The fourth shows the sleep hospital where Nancy's mom takes her to in the movie. The building is actually American Jewish University located at 15600 Mulholland Drive just off the 405 Freeway.

The fifth page shows the bridge where Nancy and Glen were talking in the movie. This was filmed at the Venice Canals in Venice Beach. The bridge they were on is unique in design and easily located once you're there.

"Time Changer"

2002

Time Changer has long been one of my favorite Christian movies ever made. I first saw it in 2003 and loved it. It was filmed largely in Fresno and Visalia in California. It has many great actors such as Gavin MacLeod, Hal Linden, and Paul Rodriguez.

In the storyline Grace Bible Seminary Professor Russell Carlisle in 1890 seeks approval from the board of directors on his new book which teaches that good morals can be taught apart from Christ. He is opposed by Professor Norris Anderson (played by MacLeod). Professor Carlisle seeks a rule change concerning the need for a unanimous endorsement. He is refused a rule change and told to discuss his differences with Anderson privately.

Anderson expresses his fears that teaching morals apart from Christ will be damaging to society. To prove his point he sends Professor Carlisle over 100 years into the future via a time machine his father invented. Professor Carlisle is shocked by society in the 21st century.

The divorce rate is 50% as opposed to 5% in 1890. Children talk openly about lying to their parents, movies contain blasphemy. People are so bored in church they have extra activities to keep them going.

He starts a relationship with a laundromat worker played by Paul Rodriguez. He encourages the worker (named Eddie) to go to church and read his Bible. Two men in the church become suspicious of Professor Carlisle and begin to investigate him. They confront him as he is about to be transported back and are convinced they missed the rapture.

Once back in 1890 he confesses that he was wrong and that he will revise his book. Anderson tries to send a Bible into the future to see how far time goes into the future. The movie ends with the idea the end cannot be known or will be very soon.

The first location from this movie was the easiest to find. There is a scene where Professor Carlisle walks into a burger joint. This scene was filmed at the former Mearle's Drive In which is now called The Habit Burger. It is located at 604 South Mooney Blvd. in Visalia, California.

DRIVE THRU

Mearle's
DRIVE IN

When Professor Carlisle arrives in the future we see him sitting in an alley. The next few pages show the two alleys used in the movie. One is in Fresno and the other in Visalia.

The first page shows the place he was sitting as he arrived in the future. The only thing missing is the dumpster that was next to him. This is in an alley in Visalia just off of Church Street, a block south of Main Street on the West side of the street.

The second page shows a view down the alley as seen in the movie. The third page shows the buildings as he emerges from the alley. This was not filmed in the same alley. This was filmed in Fresno on Fresno Street across from Courthouse Park.

The building he is peeking around is the Crocker Building at 2135 Fresno Street. The building behind him is a Wells Fargo Bank building. The fourth page shows the Crest Theatre located at 1711 Broadway Plaza. On the corner of Broadway and Fresno Street.

Rick Garland

WELLS
FARGO

Rick Garland

On the next two pages are pictures of the laundromat which played such a prominent role in the movie. Professor Carlisle befriends an employee of the laundromat played by Paul Rodriguez.

The inside of the building is seen several times. The Professor encourages Eddie to seek the Lord and read his Bible. He asks Eddie for the name of a church he could attend in town. Eddie hands him the yellow pages which is completely foreign to the time traveler.

By the end of the movie Professor Carlisle shares the Gospel with Eddie. He promises to start reading his Bible as the visitor had asked him to do previously. The last we see of Eddie he is sitting behind his counter reading the book of Genesis.

The scenes were filmed at the Bubbles & Bleach Laundromat located at 2621 South Mooney Blvd. in Visalia. The place looks exactly the same as in the movie even the same counter that was used in the movie is still there.

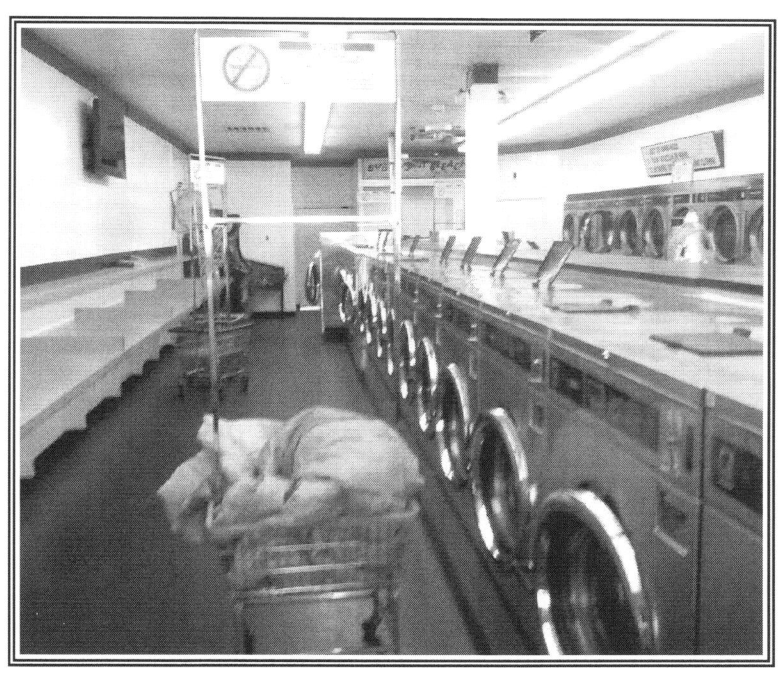

n Fold
AP
ACH
TENERS

Suds

The next few pages show the church Professor Carlisle attended in the movie. The outside and the inside of the church building are seen. Professor Carlisle is greatly troubled by the entertainment, apathy, and uninterest found in the church in the future. At the end of the movie he gives a wonderful sermon that should honestly be given in every church in America today.

The church used was called First Baptist Church of Visalia at the time. Today it is called Gateway Church of Visalia. It is located in the same location at 1100 South Sowell Street in Visalia.

The church looks pretty much identical to the movie. With only slight changes around the platform I would say the rest of it looks identical to the movie. I dropped by on a Sunday afternoon when no services were going on but was thrilled to find the doors open as they had other activities going on that day.

ENTRANCE

WORSHIP CENTER

In the movie Professor Carlisle goes on an outing with the church. They go to see a movie at a local theatre which was called “Signature Theatre.” Professor Carlisle is so struck by what he sees on the screen that he runs out and demands that they stop the movie.

The staff of the theatre just stares as he has a fit over the movie they were playing. This really begins a long process of him realizing that you cannot teach morality apart from the teachings of Jesus as he had taught in his book. He becomes grateful for this look into the future that Professor Anderson gave him.

The theatre is only a block away from the alley he finds himself in after arriving in the future. In fact, if you watch closely you can see the theater building in the movie while he looks at the newspaper in the alley. Today it is called the Regal Cinemas Stadium 10 located at 120 South Bridge in Visalia.

REGAL CINEMAS STADIUM 10

On the next few pages we see Courthouse Park in downtown Fresno. This area can be seen very well in the movie. The first page is a fountain that can be seen in the background several times.

The second page shows the benches that professor Carlisle is sitting on to eat his hotdog. The bench is between the building and the fountain. There are two benches by each other and a lamp post next to the bench.

The third page shows a staircase that can be seen in the background of the shot. These stairs lead under the street and access the Fulton Mall. If you're hunting this area these stairs take you right to more filming locations in the mall area.

The fourth page shows the trees of the park where Professor Carlisle chases the little girl who steals his hotdog. If you're in the area and like the movie I totally recommend taking a stroll through the park and yes, buying a hotdog, because there is always a cart there selling them.

Rick Garland

GRAND OPENING

Rick Garland

Below is a picture of the pawn shop where professor Carlisle takes his coins from the past to get money for them. I couldn't go in and disrupt business to get a picture. If you hunt here feel free to stop inside and see it for yourself.

It's just around the corner from the Fulton Mall. The pawn shop is Majestic Jewelry and Loan. The address is 1924 Tulare Street in Downtown Fresno.

Below is a picture of the department store where Professor Carlisle confronts the manager about the clothing that a mannequin is wearing. The section where this happened is still there and in the same spot. When you walk into the store the counter and section is just to your right.

This was filmed inside of the JC Penney store in the Visalia Mall. The address is 2031 South Mooney Blvd. In Visalia.

A few of the shots in the movie were filmed at the Fulton Mall in Downtown Fresno. Fulton is a six block outdoor pedestrian mall. On the next page is the clock tower which is a beautiful piece of art. If you follow the stairs from Courthouse Park it brings you into the mall right in front of the clock.

The second page shows a water fountain where Professor Carlisle gets a drink of water. It's near the clock so it's easy to locate. If you hunt this location you can pretty much walk to all of the “Time Changer” locations in the area.

The third page is the building used for the Grace Bible Seminary in the movie. I got the back of the building but it's definitely the same one. This was filmed at Fresno City College located at 1101 E. University Avenue in Fresno.

Finishing off this movie on the fourth page is a picture of the courtyard at the seminary where the professors are talking.

Rick Garland

“Duel”

1971

A duel is about to begin
between a man, a truck and
an open road.
Where a simple battle of wits
is now a matter of life and death.
DUEL

This movie follows David Mann who is a middle aged salesman driving a red 1971 Plymouth Valiant on a business trip. He encounters a grimy 1955 tanker truck going slower than the speed limit. Mann passes the truck which then speeds past him then slows down again. Mann is startled when the truck gives off a long horn honk after being passed twice.

Mann gets to a gas station and is followed by the truck. He phones his wife and has his car refueled. He is advised that he needs a new radiator hose but he refuses to get it repaired.

Once both men are back on the road the truck blocks his path when he attempts to pass it. The truck driver waves him on as if to pass only to narrowly miss an oncoming vehicle. Mann realizes the driver is trying to kill him.

Mann crashes into a guardrail across the road from a diner but the truck keeps going. Mann goes into the diner and after returning from the restroom notices the truck parked outside. He begins a dialogue with himself and begins to question which of the customers the driver of the truck is.

One customer leaves appearing to go to the truck and is confronted by Mann. The man is angry at the accusation and a fist fight takes place. After the fight the man leaves in a livestock truck and then the tanker leaves which shows the driver was never in the restaurant.

Mann stops to help a school bus and his bumper becomes stuck underneath the back of the bus. He sees the truck at the end of the tunnel and goes into a panic. He frees his car and manages to leave but then becomes confused to see the truck stop to help.

While at a railroad crossing the truck tries to push Mann into an oncoming train. The train passes just in time and Mann crosses and pulls over. When Mann finds the truck again it is sitting there as though waiting for him.

Mann pulls into a gas station for fuel and to call the police. The truck plows into the phone booth that he is using. Mann jumps clear just in time.

The truck chases Mann (who is on foot). It destroys the gas station releasing rattlesnakes housed on the property. Mann hides as the truck passes by him. He gets back into his car only to find the truck waiting for him.

He tries to approach the truck on foot but it keeps moving away from him. He tries to get help from a passerby but they think he is crazy until they see the truck themselves. Once back in his car the truck allows him to pass thus beginning a high speed chase.

In the end the truck drives off a cliff. The movie ends with Mann sitting exhausted as the sun sets. A black liquid is seen dripping from the steering wheel of the truck.

Much of the movie is filmed in Canyon Country in Southern California. Most of the places are still there and intact. The picture on the next page is the tunnel used in the movie. It can be found on Soledad Canyon Road near Canyon Country.

The second page is the restaurant where Mann goes in to get some relief only to find the truck outside waiting for him. The address is 12625 Sierra Highway in Santa Clarita.

“Liar Liar”

1997

This movie was another favorite, especially with the terrific cast. Jim Carrey plays Fletcher Reed, a Los Angeles attorney with a lying problem. His son Max is heartbroken that his dad always lies to him and his mom Audrey.

Fletcher's habit of lying has built him a reputation for being one of the best defense lawyers. He is quickly moving up the ladder of success. Audrey is troubled that Fletcher never has time for Max and that he breaks his promises to him.

When Fletcher misses his son's 5th birthday party, Max takes matters into his own hands. He wishes that his father cannot tell a lie for one whole day. His wish comes true.

Fletcher discovers through a series of embarrassing incidents that he cannot lie, mislead, or even withhold a true answer. He discovers that he cannot even ask a question if he knows the answer will be a lie, which hurts his career.

Audrey is planning to move Max to Boston to protect him from being hurt by Fletcher. At the same time Fletcher is working on a divorce case that could really make his career. His new condition puts a huge burden on his case.

He tries to delay the case but to no avail. He even beats himself up in an attempt to delay the case. He finds out that his client had lied about her age in her prenuptial agreement thus rendering it invalid.

This helps him to realize what he is about to lose himself if Max leaves. His client reveals that she only cares about her husband's money and wants to take the kids away from him to get more money. This leads Fletcher to call for the judge to reverse his decision which leads to Fletcher being arrested for contempt of court.

After Audrey refuses to pay his bail he is bailed out by his secretary. He rushes to the airport to stop them from leaving but the plane has already left the gate. He hijacks a mobile staircase and goes after the plane. He does stop it but is injured in the process. He vows to make Max his highest priority and to stop lying. Audrey decides not to move to Boston.

The house from the movie is very beautiful and looks much the same as it did at the time of filming. It is located at 1004 Highland Avenue in South Pasadena. **This is a private residence so please respect their privacy and do not trespass.**

ANNE HANEY

“Return To Mayberry”

1986

Based on the television show, this movie follows Andy Taylor (who is now a U.S. Postal Inspector) as he returns to his hometown of Mayberry, North Carolina. His arrival comes in the wake of his son Opie having his first child. He plans on running for sheriff once again in Mayberry and even has the paperwork ready on his arrival.

Andy soon learns that his former deputy (and cousin) Barney Fife is running and he puts aside his plans. Barney had moved back after leaving for Raleigh, North Carolina. Barney is now the sheriff but only having been appointed by the last sheriff. He hopes to win the position on his own.

The only real hitch is that the people of the town think he has lost his sanity. He falls for a publicity stunt which starts a rumor that there is a monster in nearby Myers Lake. At the same time Opie, the editor of the newspaper, contemplates moving his family out of Mayberry.

Most of the old characters from the television show returned for this one with a few exceptions. Andy solves the mystery of the lake monster and makes it appear as though Barney solved the mystery. Barney and Thelma Lou finally tie the knot at the end as well.

At a “Fife victory rally” Barney learns that Andy

withdrew from the race for sheriff. He gives an emotional withdrawal from the race and supports Andy. The movie ends with Sheriff Andy Taylor and Deputy Barney Fife folding a flag on the main street of Mayberry.

The sets for "The Andy Griffith Show" had long been torn down by the time this movie was filmed. To recreate the small North Carolina town they turned to a small town called Los Olivos, California. This town is located between Santa Maria and Buellton along the California central coast.

All of the buildings are still there and very much recognizable. Walking through this little town is like walking through the real Mayberry and townspeople are very friendly.

I don't include addresses because the town is small and quaint enough to walk and see all of the locations used. I suggest you take time to visit if you're in the area. I will give general directions when I can.

On the next page is the place where they set up the fake Mayberry courthouse. The false building was set up around a little park along the main street. The second page shows a building right next to the courthouse. This building is still very recognizable from the movie.

Jedlicka's

Hubacher's Hardware

The next location that can be seen is Opie's office door. The door and building are still intact and very easily recognized today. It is directly across the street from the park where the false courthouse stood.

On the second page is the front part of the same building. It is seen clearly when Andy and the town clerk Howard are standing around talking. It is directly across from the park.

The third page shows the flagpole which is seen in the middle of the town. There was no flagpole seen in the original show, but it certainly adds a bit of small town flavor in the movie. It was the first thing I recognized as I came into town.

The fourth page shows the building that was Gomer and Goober's Garage. This was a hard one to find but definitely worth it. There is a new building in front of it but the location is the same.

The fifth page shows Myers Lake. This was filmed at the Upper Franklin Canyon Reservoir in Beverly Hills.

WINE
TASTING

G & G GARAGE
GAS
GAS

On the next page is a picture of the building that Andy is standing in front of while waiting for Helen to arrive on the bus. This building, like most of the locations from this movie, is just a stone's throw from the flagpole in the center of town. There is a building next to it now (there wasn't in the movie), but otherwise it's very much the same as it was.

The second page shows the place where the fake cemetery was when Andy went to visit Aunt Bea's grave. This is actually the back of a church there in town. The only way we found it was by the black fence which is still there. We also took notice of the view of the white church in the background of the movie. My wife is actually the brilliant mind who found this one.

UMABLE ART IN LOS OLIVOS
WINE TASTING

To finish off this movie is a picture of the church where Barney and Thelma Lou were married in the movie. This is actually a cute little country church called Berean Baptist Church.

The Knickerbocker Hotel at 1714 Ivar Avenue has been part of the Hollywood legend for decades. Elvis Presley stayed here while filming his first movie "Love Me Tender" in 1956 and studio head D.W. Griffith passed out in the lobby before dying on the way to the hospital. Marilyn Monroe, Joe Dimaggio, Rudolph Valentino and others would gather at the bar and interact with fans.

"Cheaper By the Dozen"

2003

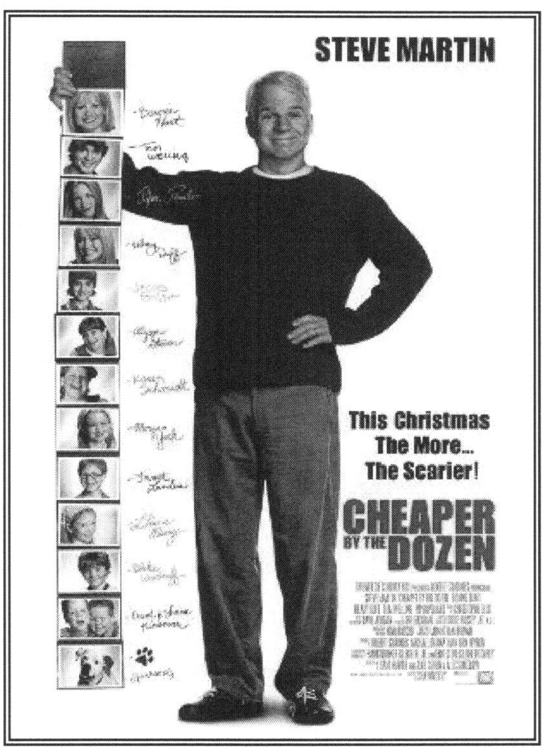

This (as always) is a great Steve Martin movie. Kate Baker narrates the story of her large family which includes her husband Tom, (a football coach) and their 12 children.

Kate wrote the family story in a book which she hoped to publish. Tom receives a job offer which would move the family from Midland, Indiana to Evanston, Illinois. He accepts the position and has the children vote on moving. He loses the vote but the move comes anyway.

They were given a large mansion, but all the room doesn't help the atmosphere. Trouble looms for all the children between fighting at home and adjusting to the new school environment. It's a time of chaos for the family.

When Kate's book is ready for publication she finds out that she has to go on tour to promote the book. Tom assures her that he can handle the household on his own. He decides to hire his oldest daughter Nora, and her child hating boyfriend Hank played by Ashton Kutcher.

Hank is reluctant since the kids had previously set his pants on fire, but he does go along. The kids begin to target Hank. This causes Nora and Hank to take off. Tom now realizes he can't handle it but it's too late because Kate is gone.

Tom tries to hire a housekeeper, but is unable to find one due to the size of the family. Tom involves the football team and mixes preparing the team with running the household which leads to yet more chaos. Kate overhears about the trouble and cancels her book tour.

The publisher decides to film a segment with Oprah Winfrey at the Baker house. They are unable to demonstrate the love and bonding that she portrayed in her book and the segment is cancelled. A huge fight erupts right before the segment and one of the children runs away from home.

A search ensues and the child is found trying to return to their old home. Tom finally decides to quit and take a job that allows him more time with the family. The movie ends with Kate narrating and the family celebrating Christmas dinner.

The house used in the movie is a large beautiful house. It is located in the lovely Hancock Park neighborhood of Los Angeles. The house is very much the same as in the movie. The address is 357 South Lorraine Blvd. **This is a private residence so please respect their privacy and do not trespass.**

BEKINS

"A Lot Like Love"

2005

This movie is presented as a series of chapters and each transpires at a turning point in the life of the character. Emily meets Oliver (played by Ashton Kutcher) on a flight from Los Angeles, to New York City. He is a budding internet entrepreneur and tells her to call him in six years to see if his visions of success come true.

The scene moves to three years in the future and Emily calls Oliver as opposed to spending New Year's Eve alone. They have dinner together. The two move in and out of other relationships and continue to reunite with each other.

To make a long story short in the end they both realize that they are meant for each other. They figure out that they will bring each other fulfillment. The place I have visited is from the cemetery scene.

The scene was filmed at Mountain View Cemetery in Altadena, California. The grave from the movie is fake but the location can be found by looking at nearby markers. It took me over an hour to find the right spot. The area it is in is labeled 4474.

Rick Garland

The Brown Derby Plaza *located at 3427 Wilshire Blvd. is built on the location of the original Brown Derby Restaurant.*

"Pretty Woman"

1990

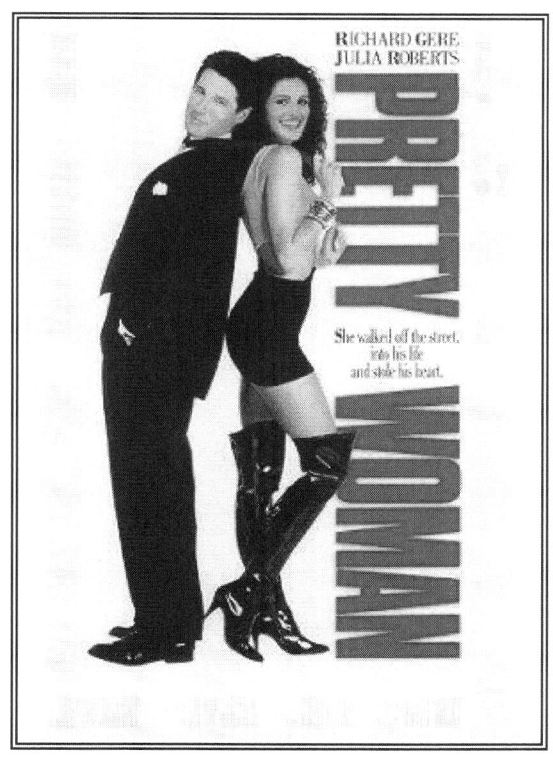

Richard Gere and Julia Roberts star in this timeless classic. Edward Lewis is a corporate raider who stops to ask for directions along Hollywood Blvd. He meets a hooker named Vivian who offers to help him with directions as long as he pays her. Her friend Kit tries to convince her to make him part of her regular customers.

Edward hires Vivian to pose as his girlfriend for a week. She agrees to do it for the sum of $3,000. He gives her the use of his credit cards as well as part of the deal. During this time Vivian falls in love with Edward (which she admits to after he takes a day off to spend with her).

Edward offers to put her into an apartment so that he can keep seeing her, but she is insulted by this. She claims this arrangement is not the fairy tale she wants. He changes his mind on his business dealings as Vivian has shown him a different view of life.

He tries to persuade her to stay but instead she returns to the apartment she shares with her friend Kit. She plans on moving to San Francisco to seek a better life. He gets into his limo, but goes to her apartment rather than the airport.

Vivian had described her favorite childhood fantasy to him (which was the knight rescuing the princess from the tower). He climbs up the fire escape with flowers to woo her and rescue her. The movie ends with them kissing on the fire escape.

There are a few spots from this movie that I have been to. The next page shows the house where Edward (Richard Gere) asks for directions to Beverly Hills. The guy points to this house and says it is Sylvester Stallone's house.

The house is pretty much the same as it appears in the movie. It is located just off Hollywood Blvd. The address is 1735 North Hudson. **This is a private residence so please respect their privacy and do not trespass.**

The second page shows the building where they are seen having dinner in the movie. It appears to be a restaurant called "Barb's Quickie Grill." It was a gray building in the movie, but it was actually a smaller structure built in front of an existing structure.

The building today is orange, but you can tell it is the same building with the smaller structure removed. It is located at 7006 Santa Monica Blvd. In Hollywood.

Rick Garland

The next page is a picture of The Outpost Building located at 6715 Hollywood Blvd. I have not yet been able to get there when the building is open but good luck if you try.

This building was originally an apartment house for aspiring Hollywood actors but today is an office building. It stood in for the alleyway that Julia Roberts is walking through at the beginning of the movie when the body of a fellow prostitute is pulled from a dumpster.

The second page is of the Blue Banana Club from the movie. Vivian goes after walking through the alley. The building is right next to the Egyptian Theatre although in the movie it is said to be next to a different one. The building is located at 6708 Hollywood Blvd.

The third page is of the apartment building where Vivian and Kit lived. The fire escape where Edward and Vivian kiss is part of the actual building. It is located just off of Hollywood Blvd. It belongs to the Las Palmas Hotel at 1738 North Las Palmas Ave.

IAN

Blue
CLUB
THEATRE I

OTEL

On the next two pages you will see the fountain which Julia Roberts and Richard Gere visit in the movie as well as the little park where you see them on the grass. I didn't realize at first that these were in the same location.

It took me a lot of looking to find this location, but I recognized it instantly. This is located in Downtown Los Angeles near City Hall. They are actually located between the Los Angeles County Municipal Court located at 111 North Hill Street and the Kenneth Hahn Hall of Administration located at 500 West Temple Street.

“Back to the Future”

1985

This movie is the classic of classics. I have never met a person who has not watched this movie. Michael J Fox and others (including Crispin Glover and Christopher Lloyd) team up in this 1980's gem.

The setting is Hill Valley, California and the year is 1985. Marty McFly is a youth who longs to be a music legend. His family however, is made up of an alcoholic mother, a weak father who is constantly bullied by his boss Biff, and a brother and sister who are less than successful.

In the middle of the night, Marty meets his eccentric scientist friend Doctor Emmet Brown in a mall parking lot to see a new invention. Doc shows Marty a time machine which he has built out of a DeLorean. The car sports a flux capacitor, which is what makes time travel possible and plutonium, which has been stolen from Libyan terrorists.

Doc demonstrates the process for time travel by typing in the date that he invented the flux capacitor (which was November 5, 1955). Libyan terrorists attack Doc and Marty killing Doc. Marty takes off in the car.

Running from the terrorists who pursue, Marty accidently passes the threshold of 88mph. He is transported back to November 5, 1955. He begins to wander his hometown in this new era as he doesn't have enough plutonium to get back home.

While in the past, he meets his father (who is now a teenager) as well as Biff (who is a teenage bully). He disrupts the meeting between his father and mother and she becomes infatuated with Marty instead.

He finds the Doc Brown of 1955 to seek his help in getting back to the future. Doc Brown tells him that the only way to get the power he needs is to be struck by a bolt of lightning.

Marty remembers that a bolt of lightning will strike the town's clock tower on a certain date, and they decide to harness that power to get Marty back to 1985. In the meantime Marty must get his parents together, or lose his own existence.

During this time Marty has to fight off Biff and his gang as well as tell Doc that he gets killed on the night Marty came to the past. Doc refuses to listen. Marty develops a plan to get his parents together.

He finally does get them together at a school dance and his dad knocks out Biff in the process, thus gaining confidence. Marty uses the lightning and gets back to

1985 just before Doc gets killed, but fails to save him. Doc survives the gunfire by wearing a bullet proof vest. He then reveals to Marty that he read the note Marty left him 1955.

Marty finds that the events of the past have changed the future. His brother and sister are now successful and his dad is an author who hired Biff to work for him. Definitely an 80's classic.

I recommend getting the 30th anniversary collection where they have great behind the scenes stuff including deleted scenes. The scene where Marty poses as Darth Vader was actually much longer. It's so good it's too bad they cut most of it. Did you know the movie was originally set to be called "Spaceman from Pluto?" It was, and those kind of neat facts make this anniversary collection totally worth getting.

On the next page you will see the exterior used for Doc Brown's 1955 mansion. This was filmed at the Gamble house in Pasadena. The address is 4 Westmoreland Place. The property does provide guided tours and is a beautiful house and property.

The second page is pictures of the garage at the Gamble house. In terms of this house, not much has changed from the filming. It looks pretty much identical.

The third page shows what looks like the entrance to the mall when Marty arrives on skateboard. It's not a street access as it looks in the movie. It's just a driveway leading to other parts of the shopping center.

1640

STOP
STOP

ROSS

The next page shows the parking lot used as the twin pines mall in the movie. They needed a parking lot big enough to get the car going 88mph. The obvious choice was the Puente Hills Mall in City of Industry.

This mall has huge land area. The first page shows me standing where the twin pines mall sign was in the movie. The second page shows the little hill that Marty rolls down when trying to save Doc after returning from the past.

The third page shows approximately where the truck was parked when Doc unveiled the time machine. I parked my white rental car about where the truck was parked.

You will be amazed at the amount of room in this parking lot. It's clear why they chose it. The building in the background was a JC Penny in 1985, but when I visited it, it had been turned into a fitness club.

JCPenney
TWIN PINES MALL

STOP

JCPenney
TWIN PINES MALL
1:16 AM

On the next pages we will see more of the houses used in the movie. What's great is that they are all on the same street so you can park and just walk along this beautiful neighborhood and see the houses.

The first is the house of George McFly in 1955. This house is completely unchanged from the movie as far as I can tell. The house is located at 1711 Bushnell in South Pasadena. **This is a private residence so please respect their privacy and do not trespass.**

The second page shows the tree where George McFly was spying on Lorraine. He falls from the tree and Marty saves him from getting hit by a car.

The third page shows the house used as Lorraine's house. This house sits unchanged by time. You can even see the window where George was spying through in the upper right side of the house. The house is located at 1727 Bushnell. **This is a private residence so please respect their privacy and do not trespass.**

Rick Garland

On the next page we see the school used as Hill Valley High School in "Back to the Future." This was filmed at Whittier High School. This building just has a great 1955 look.

It still looks very much the same as it did in the movie. The parking lot used for the dance scene is actually a grass area, not a parking lot. They had to pull cars onto the grass to give the appearance of a parking lot. The school is located at 12417 Philadelphia Street in Whittier.

The second page is the staircase used in the dance scene of the movie. The dance scene took place in the gym at the same location but I couldn't get a picture due to a basketball game taking place. This was filmed at the Hollywood United Methodist Church located at 6817 Franklin Avenue in Hollywood.

HILL VALLEY

On the next page we see the location of the famous Hill Valley Lyon Estates sign that we see several times in the movie. They want you to think this is on the street where Marty lives but it's actually located a few blocks away.

The signs were set up on the corner of Sandusky and Kagel Canyon Road. The scene is looking southeast down Sandusky. This is located in the Arleta community of the San Fernando Valley.

The second page shows the house used as Marty's house. It is located in Arleta and looks exactly the same as in the movie. Even the power lines behind the house make it recognizable. This house is located at 9303 Roslyndale Avenue. **This is a private residence so please respect their privacy and do not trespass.**

The third and fourth pages show a scene from the opening of the movie. We see Marty leave Doc Brown's place on his skateboard. That was a temporary facade put up in a parking lot next to a Burger King. Marty skateboards from Doc Brown's place past Burger King in the movie. The address is 535 N. Victory Blvd. In Burbank.

LYON

BURGER KING

KING

The next two pages cover the gym from the battle of the bands part of the movie. This is the scene where Marty tries out for the school dance but is told by Huey Lewis that he is “just too darn loud.” This was filmed at the McCambridge Recreation Center.

This place is located at 1515 N. Glenoaks Blvd. in Burbank. It is open to the public, just check the hours of operation and show up there accordingly.

The third page is the starting point for the DeLorean when Marty was heading back to the future. This was accomplished via a lightning strike from the clock tower. It looks like Marty is on the backlot at Universal, but it's not.

It was filmed in Griffith Park just across the street from the Greek Theatre. Look for the spot where there is a funny shaped tree, a light post, and a bench.

"we the people"
AUDITIONS BATTLE OF THE BANDS
YAMAHA

BLUEBIRD
MOTEL

"A Nightmare on Elm Street Part 2: Freddy's Revenge"

1985

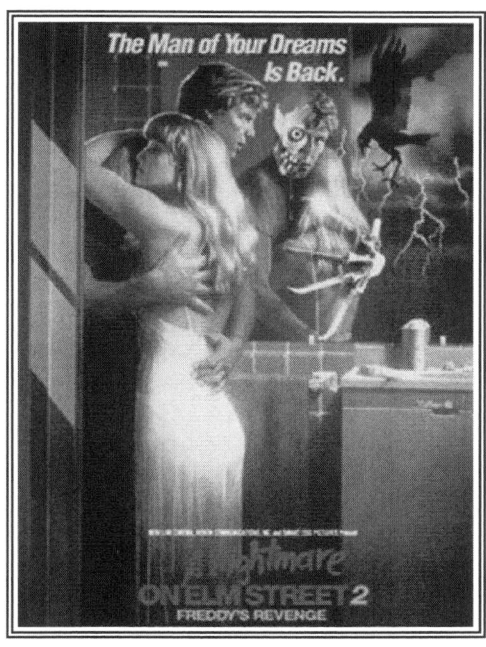

This second Nightmare movie is set 5 years after the first one. They use the same house as in the first one, but I won't include it again. There are plenty of other locations to see.

The Walsh family moves into Nancy Thompson's old house. The oldest child, Jesse, moves into Nancy's old room and soon begins having nightmares. Freddy Krueger stalks Jesse and demands that Jesse allow him to use his body to kill.

Jesse's girlfriend Lisa finds Nancy's diary in the closet. The diary chronicles her encounters with Krueger which explains the situation to both of them. Krueger begins to take possession of Jesse's body and to kill. After each killing it goes from showing Freddy to showing Jesse wearing Krueger's glove.

After killing his friend Grady, Jesse runs to Lisa's house where a pool party is taking place. He is once again taken over by Freddy and begins to kill there as partygoers try to attack Freddy. After cornering the crowd he disappears into a fire ball.

Lisa goes to the old mill where Fred Krueger once worked and took his victims. She finds Freddy/Jesse and tells him to fight from the inside. She takes off Freddy's hat and kisses him.

Freddy loses control while the power plant begins to burn. Freddy starts burning and after he dies the fire in the plant is stopped. When Lisa thinks it's all over Freddy's corpse begins to move and Jesse crawls out of the ashes.

On the next page is a picture of the school used in the movie as Springwood High School. It is actually an adult school but formerly it was the Charles Evans Hughes Junior High. It is located at 5607 Capistrano Avenue in Woodland Hills.

On the second page you will see the corner where people are standing in the beginning of the movie when the school bus passes by. This corner is located in Palmdale at E. Ave. R12 and Mahonia Avenue.

The third page shows the field where the bus drives off into the desert. This can be found at E. Ave. S and 51st Street in Palmdale. The fourth page shows a scene where the bus was driving in the movie.

SCHOOLBUS

*The **Capitol Records Building** at 1750 Vine Street in Hollywood. This building has been a staple of Hollywood for many years, being visited by many celebrities including Elvis Presley and Frank Sinatra.*

"Back To The Future: Part 2"

1989

The day after Marty returns to 1985 Doc Brown returns from a trip to the year 2015. He tells Marty that he and his girlfriend Jennifer must come with him to the future to help their son avoid jail. Biff witnesses their departure in a flying DeLorean.

Doc gives Jennifer a sedative and leaves her asleep in an alley while Marty poses as his son in order to reject the chance to help Biff's grandson Griff in a robbery. This robbery was the cause of his son's imprisonment. The plan backfires and Griff and his gang draw Marty into a fight.

After a short chase Griff and his gang crash into the courthouse and are arrested. Marty buys a sports Almanac before meeting back up with Doc. This book outlines the winning team in sporting events from 1950 to 2000.

Doc warns Marty of the dangers of the book. Before he can throw it away they are interrupted by the police picking up who they think is the Jennifer of the future. They figure she is drunk and take her home.

Biff as an old man hears about the time machine and the Almanac. Doc drops the Almanac into the trash and follows the police. Biff takes the Almanac and follows in a cab.

While Marty and Doc rescue Jennifer from her future house Biff takes the time machine. He travels back to 1955 and gives the Almanac to his younger self. Marty, Jennifer and Doc return to 1985 not realizing what Biff has done.

The time travelers find that the 1985 they have returned to is far different than the one they left. Biff is now rich and corrupt and runs the city of Hill Valley. Doc is in an asylum, George McFly is dead having been murdered and Biff forced Lorraine to marry him.

Doc and Marty discover evidence that Biff stole the time machine to give himself the Almanac and change the past. Marty confronts Biff who admits that an old man gave him an Almanac on November 12, 1955. He tells Marty that he is the one who shot and killed his father. Doc rescues Marty just before Biff can shoot him as well.

The two of them escape to 1955. Marty follows Biff and watches him get the Almanac from his future self. He chases Biff causing him to eventually crash his car into a manure truck.

Marty burns the Almanac on the ground as Doc hovers overhead in the DeLorean. This fixes the problems caused by Biff. Before the two can return to the future the

DeLorean is struck by lightning and disappears with Doc.

Just after this happens a man from Western Union arrives and gives Marty a 79 year old letter from Doc. The letter reveals that the lightning strike sent him back to 1885. Marty rushes to get the help of the 1955 Doc Brown who only seconds earlier had sent the Marty from the first movie back to 1985.

On the next page is a picture of the house shown as Biff's house in the movie. Aside from the gate and all the junk being gone there is not much of a difference. Even the railings on the porch are the same.

This house is located on the same street as the houses for Lorraine and George in the first movie. The address is 1809 Bushnell in South Pasadena. **This is a private residence so please respect their privacy and do not trespass.**

Rick Garland

The next page shows the tunnel used in the chase scene. The tunnel is much shorter than it appears in the movie. This is due to camera effects. The tunnel is located in Griffith Park on the way up the hill to the Observatory.

The second page shows the house where Biff throws a ball which he took from some kids in the movie. The ball lands on a little balcony section of the house. This house is located on the same street as the others from this movie series. The address is 1803 Bushnell in South Pasadena. **This is a private residence so please respect their privacy and do not trespass.**

The next page shows the house used as Jennifer's house in the movie. This house took me some time to find as it's not near the other ones at all. This house is amazingly the same as in the movie even to the point of the porch swing.

The address is 161 North Magnolia in Monrovia. The property owners deserve privacy. If you visit this house park across the street and take photos from a distance. Do not go on the property for the swing. The swing is visible from the street. **This is a private residence so please respect their privacy and do not trespass.**

On the second page is another great location from this movie. It is the house used as Mr. Strickland's house. Marty ends up there in the alternate 1985.

This house is located within sight of the high school in Whittier. The only real difference is that in the movie the stairs are in the front of the porch leading to the door and now they are on the side of the porch. Otherwise the house is identical.

The house is located at 12511 Bailey Street in Whittier. **This is a private residence so please respect their privacy and do not trespass.**

On the next few pages you will see the stairwell where Marty is chased by Biff's cronies in the alternate 1985. I found this location thanks to bttftour.com. You will notice the strange staircase because it has two staircases side by side which allowed Marty to jump from one staircase to the other.

On the first page is the spot where Marty jumps over the railing the first time, the second page shows the door he came out of, the third page shows him jumping back over the railing, and the fourth shows the roof access door he used.

These scenes were shot in the 3rd level of the underground parking at the Hilton Hotel at Universal Studios. To see it you have to pay to park. Go to the third level and go into the staircase on the far left of the parking area.

EXIT

ROOF
ROOF ACCESS

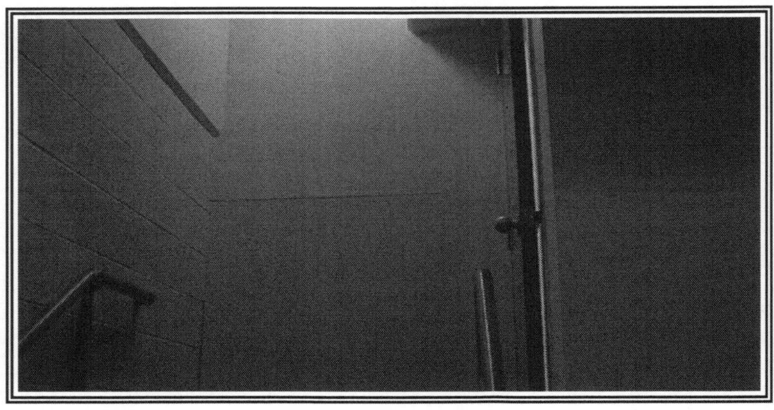

"A Nightmare on Elm Street Part 3: Dream Warriors"

1987

This third installment of the Nightmare series centers on a girl named Kristen Parker. She has a dream where Freddy cuts her wrists. When she wakes up the cuts are real but her mom thinks that she is trying to kill herself and has her put into a hospital.

Kristen becomes hysterical when the staff try to sedate her. She is calmed by Nancy Thompson (from the first movie) who now works as a dream therapist. Nancy finishes the nursery rhyme that Kristen hears. Nancy also recognizes a model of her old house which helps her gain Kristen's trust.

There are other patients at the hospital, all experiencing the same nightmares. They are all under the care of a man named Neil. He has been trying to convince them that their dreams won't hurt them.

Kristen has another nightmare about Freddy. During the encounter, she is able to pull Nancy into her dream. Nancy saves Kristen from Freddy who immediately recognizes Nancy.

Nancy makes an attempt to get Neil to prescribe a medication to suppress their dreams, but he refuses. One of the patients has a dream where Freddy makes him fall from the top of the building. The staff assumes it was a suicide.

Another patient stays up late against the rules to watch television. The orderly allows her to because she is mourning her friend's death. Freddy comes out of the television and kills her as well.

Following this death, Nancy tells the others who Freddy is. She explains that they are being targeted because they are the last of the Elm Street children. She tells them that Kristen's ability to bring people into her dreams is the advantage they need to beat Freddy.

Nancy and Neil organize a group dream through hypnosis. The group realizes that while dreaming they have special abilities. Nancy describes these as battling abilities they can use to fight Freddy on his turf.

During the dream one of the group wanders off and gets into an encounter with Freddy. Freddy ties him to a bed and dangles him over a pit of fire. When the group wakes up they find that he is in a coma.

As a result of the coma and the suggestion of the sleep suppression both Neil and Nancy are fired. Dr. Simms (who runs the ward) orders nightly sedation for the group. These events come at the same time as the appearance of a nun in white named Sister Mary Helena. She tells Neil that Freddy is the bastard son of a hundred maniacs and the only way to stop him is to lay his bones to rest.

Neil convinces Nancy to talk to her father (who is the only person who knows where Freddy's body is hidden). Her father refuses to help at first. Neil receives a page from the hospital where Kristen has been sedated and put into a special room for acting up.

Neil confronts Donald Thompson who takes Neil to get Freddy's bones. Nancy returns to the hospital for a group dream session to fight Freddy. Kristen is able to pull Nancy and the others into her dream.

The group gets split up and two of them are killed individually. The rest of the group join forces to battle Freddy who disappears just as his bones are laid to rest. Freddy possesses his remains and kills Donald while injuring Neil.

Freddy then returns to the dream world to fight Nancy and the others. It looks as though the group defeats Freddy. The spirit of Nancy's father appears and tells Nancy that he has crossed over. While the two embrace it's revealed that the spirit is really Freddy who then stabs Nancy.

Kristen attempts to kill Freddy on her own. Nancy comes from behind and stabs Freddy with his own glove just as Neil in the real world throws holy water and a cross on Freddy's bones. Freddy is killed as Nancy dies in Kristen's arms.

During Nancy's funeral Neil sees Sister Mary Helena in the cemetery and goes to speak with her. When he arrives where he saw the nun, she is gone. He sees a tombstone dedicated to Mary Helena-Amanda Krueger. This reveals that the nun was actually the mother of Freddy.

The movie ends with Neil asleep and by him Kristen's model of 1428 Elm Street. As Neil sleeps, the bedroom light in the model comes on showing that Freddy is still alive.

The building used for the hospital in the movie is actually Royce Hall, on the campus of UCLA. On the next few pages you will see comparison shots of the building used in the movie.

“Valentine's Day”

2010

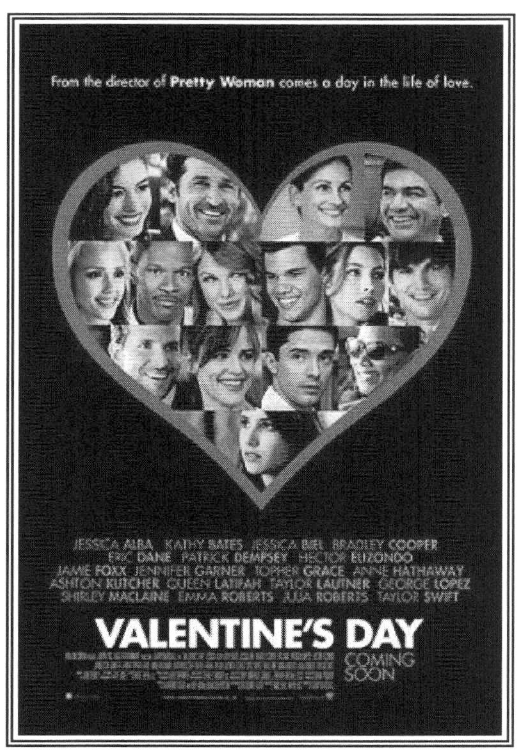

This is an excellent movie filled with stars. It opens with a florist named Reed (played by Ashton Kutcher) who wakes up and proposes to his girlfriend Morely (played by Jessica Alba). She accepts his proposal. Reed's closest friends Alfonso and Julia (played by George Lopez and Jennifer Garner) are surprised she accepts, but not surprised when she dumps him a few hours later.

Kate is an Army captain (played by Julia Roberts) who is seen on a flight to Los Angeles. She meets Holden (played by Bradley Cooper). She is making a very long trip for such a very short visit. After landing, Holden offers her a ride in his limousine rather than waiting hours for a taxi.

Julia is a school teacher who has fallen in love with a doctor named Harrison (played by Patrick Dempsey). He is cheating on his wife Pamela. He tells Julia that he has to go to San Francisco on business.

On his way, Harrison stops by Reed's flower shop revealing to Reed that he is having an affair. Reed warns Julia, but she flies to San Francisco against his warnings. Julia dresses as a waitress at a local restaurant and causes a scene while Harrison is at lunch with his wife.

The movie then begins to circle around several different situations. A student in Julia's class named Edison (played by Bryce Robinson) orders flowers from Reed. The flowers are for Julia but she suggests that Edison give them to Rani which is a girl in class who likes him.

Edison's babysitter Grace (played by Emma Roberts) plans to sleep with her boyfriend Alex (played by Carter Jenkins). This is foiled when her mom finds him naked in Grace's bedroom. This leads to an awkward (but hilarious) exit from Grace's house by Alex.

Edison's grandparents are facing marital troubles. His grandmother Estelle (played by the fabulous Shirley MacLaine) admits to having cheated on her husband Edgar (played by Hector Elizondo). She regrets the action, but he has trouble getting past it.

Grace's friends have used Valentine's Day to go the opposite way she is. Willy and Felicia (played by Taylor Lautner and Taylor Swift) have decided to wait to have sex. In my opinion Taylor Swift's elevator scene is one of the funniest of the movie.

Just when you think you have seen all the stars and plot twists you can for one movie, there is more. Sean Jackson (played by Eric Dane) is a pro football player who is in the closet and facing the end of his career. His publicist is Kara (played by Jessica Biel) and his agent is Paula (played by Queen Latifah).

Kara is organizing an annual "I Hate Valentine's Day" party. The only problem is her interest in Kelvin. He is a news reporter (played by Jamie Foxx). He was given instructions to do a news story on Valentine's Day by his boss Susan (played by Kathy Bates). Kelvin hates Valentine's Day as much as Kara.

Paula hires a new receptionist named Liz (played by Anne Hathaway). She is seeing a man in the mail room named Jason (played by Topher Grace). He is surprised to find out that Liz also works as a phone sex operator to pay off a student loan. Jason has trouble coping with such news until he is inspired by Edgar who forgives Estelle.

Sean does come out of the closet. Kate (from the beginning of the movie) arrives home, but it's to see her son Edison not her lover. Grace and Alex agree to wait to have sex and Edgar and Estelle renew their marriage vows and reconcile their relationship.

Pamela leaves the cheating Harrison. Morely tries to call Reed. Unfortunately for her, he is starting a new relationship with Julia. All in a day's work you might say concerning this movie.

I have been to several locations from this movie as it was filmed all over the Los Angeles area. The first is the house that Reed and Morely live in at the start of the film. You can see on the next page that the house has not changed.

The house Reed lived in and the yellow house next to it are both seen in the movie. The address is 2604 Grand Canal in Venice Beach. **This is a private residence so please respect their privacy and do not trespass.**

This was my first visit to the Venice Canals and it was worth it. If you have not been there before, stroll the area after seeing the house. On the next page you will see Reed's house from the movie.

The second page is of the bridge where George Lopez's character was waiting for Reed. The third page shows the view George Lopez had from the bridge (which is also seen at the end when Reed and Julia kiss). What's neat is that directly in front of that bridge is the bridge from "A Nightmare on Elm Street." On the fourth page you'll see where the floral van was parked. The fifth page shows the stepping stones visible just past Reed in the van.

The next page shows the Los Angeles Flower Market. It is located in the Warehouse District. The address is 754 Wall Street in Downtown Los Angeles.

The second page shows the apartment building which Harrison lived in. This is actually the Grand Tower located at 255 South Grand in Downtown Los Angeles. **This is a private residence so please respect their privacy and do not trespass.**

The third page shows the building where a worker is seen pulling up a metal door. The building is Hollywood Magic Inc. and is located at 6614 Hollywood Blvd. in Hollywood. On the fourth page you will see a large metal door depicting Lucille Ball. This building is located just down the street from Hollywood Magic.

Southern California
FLOWER MARKET

The Original Los Angeles
FLOWER MARKET

THE EMERSON
NOW LEASING
TheEmersonLA.com
213.337.9900
RELATED RENTALS

Hail-A-Taxi
St. PIERRE'S
Hollywood
MAGIC inc
Professional Magic · Fun Items · Games

Rick Garland

On the next page you will see the Walt Disney Concert Hall in Downtown Los Angeles. This is stunning architecture (as are many of the modern buildings in Southern California). Even if you haven't seen the movie this is a must see. This can be seen in the part where George Lopez gets into an accident in the delivery van. The building is located at 111 S. Grand Ave.

On the second page you will see the building where Topher Grace's office was located in the movie. This is in a very busy area of L.A. so be cautious when going here. This is the Creative Artists Agency building. The address is 2000 Avenue of the Stars in Century City.

The third and fourth pages show Hollywood Forever Cemetery. The movie is true to life as the cemetery does host movies on the wall of the mausoleum during the summer months. In this cemetery lie the remains of not only the founder of Hollywood (Harvey Wilcox), but many other notables such as: Cecile B. DeMille, Bugsy Siegel, Rudolph Valentino, Mel Blanc and many others.

The address is 6000 Santa Monica Blvd. in Hollywood.

HOLLYWOOD FOREVER
CEMETERY
FUNERAL HOME
FLOWERS & GIFTS
6000

HOLLYWOOD FOREVER
Cemetery
Funeral Home
Flowers & Gifts

HOT SPELL
... will begin in 5 minutes

On the next page you will see Henderson High School from the movie. This is where Taylor Lautner, Emma Roberts and Taylor Swift go to school. This school is actually University High School located at 11800 Texas Ave. in West Los Angeles.

The second page shows the house where Emma Roberts babysits in the movie. This house still looks exactly the same as it did in the movie. I didn't notice any differences at all. The address is 14280 Greenleaf Street in Sherman Oaks. **This is a private residence so please respect their privacy and do not trespass.**

The third page shows a car wash that Emma Roberts passes while looking for Edison. He ran away which causes her to go after him. This car wash is noticeable because of the giant hand and car used for the sign. Both are still there and intact. You can find them at Studio City Car Wash located at 11514 Ventura Blvd. in Studio City.

The last two pages show the flower shop owned by Ashton Kutcher's character. There is a store there today though not a flower shop. The "Sienna Bouquet" flower shop is located at 3100 Magnolia Blvd. in Burbank.

HAND
CAR
WASH

SIENA BOUQUET
21 78

“A Nightmare on Elm Street Part 4: Dream Master”

1988

This fourth installment of the Nightmare franchise was the highest grossing until “Freddy vs. Jason” came out in 2003. This movie is a sequel to the “Dream Warriors” movie which came before it. The three surviving members of the previous movie appear in this one... at least for a short time.

Kristen, Joey and Kincaid are living normal lives having been out of the asylum for some time. Kristen makes new friends in high school. She spends her time with Alice, Shiela, Debbie and her new boyfriend Rick. Kristen is haunted by a feeling that Freddy is not dead and will at some point come back.

Kristen pulls Joey and Kincaid into a dream with her. The dream takes place at Freddy's old house. The guys explain that the boiler is cold and empty, which means Freddy is not coming back. Kincaid's dog jumps out of the boiler and bites Kristen. When they wake up the bite appears in real life.

The next evening Kincaid dreams and finds himself in a salvage yard. This is the same yard where Freddy's bones were buried in the last movie. Freddy is resurrected and stalks Kincaid.

He is able to send cars down on Freddy but he traps

Kincaid and stabs him. Joey falls asleep on his waterbed and is tricked by Freddy who stabs him and drowns him. His mother finds him the next morning.

Kristen notices that Joey and Kincaid don't come to school and she goes into a panic. She gets knocked out and faces Freddy before the school nurse wakes her up. She tells her friends about Freddy, including Alice who knows a nursery rhyme which can help control your dreams.

Kristen's mom secretly gives her some sleeping pills which puts her in a dream in which she is talking to a little girl making a sand castle. Freddy comes up through the sand and Kristen runs into quicksand trying to escape. Freddy pushes her under the sand with his foot.

This situation forces Kristen to call Alice into her dream. As a result, Freddy is allowed access to children not from Elm Street. He throws Kristen into his boiler where she is burned alive in front of Alice. Before she dies Kristen gives her powers to Alice but they accidently pass through Freddy as well. Alice and Rick go to Kristen's house and find her burning in her room.

The next day Alice pulls Shiela into her dream and Freddy kills her. In a dream Rick faces Freddy in martial arts but Freddy cheats and kills him. Alice finds out that with each death she gains aspects of her friends' personalities and dream powers and Freddy collects their souls.

Alice, Dan and Debbie plan an attack on Freddy but Freddy turns Debbie into a roach and kills her in a roach motel. Dan gets injured in the real world and sent to the hospital. He and Alice face Freddy when he is put under but he is dragged from the dream world when the doctors bring him out of it.

Alice faces Freddy alone and uses the nursery rhyme of the dream master to allow his collected souls to revolt and tear him to shreds. Freddy's clothes fall to the ground and he appears to be dead. Later as Dan and Alice are dating they walk by a fountain and Alice sees Freddy's reflection in the water which fades as Dan's coin hits the water.

On the next page is the fountain from the movie. It is located at Los Feliz and Riverside just off Interstate 5 across from the entrance to Griffith Park in Los Angeles.

On the next page is the location used for the Crave Inn Diner in the movie. The restaurant used for filming is called Cafe Laurent. This was a good one to find because it's near so many other filming locations.

The building looks very similar to the time of the movie. The shape of the building is the same, the only real difference is the color of the building. The address is 4243 Overland Ave. in Culver City.

The second page shows Alice and Rick Johnson's house. This house looks exactly (and I mean exactly) as it did in the movie. The address is 1510 W. Oak Street in Burbank. **This is a private residence so please respect their privacy and do not trespass.**

The third page shows Kristen's house which also looks exactly as it does in the movie. There is a street light in front of the house that wasn't there in the movie but the house itself looks identical. It is located at 450 N. June Street in Hollywood. **This is a private residence so please respect their privacy and do not trespass.**

LAURENT

On the next page you can see the school used as Springwood High School for this movie. Each movie seems to use a different location for the school. The shots were filmed at Venice High School in Venice. The address is 13000 Venice Blvd.

On the second page you can see the Rialto Theatre which was used in a dream sequence in the movie. This is located at 1023 Fair Oaks Ave. in South Pasadena.

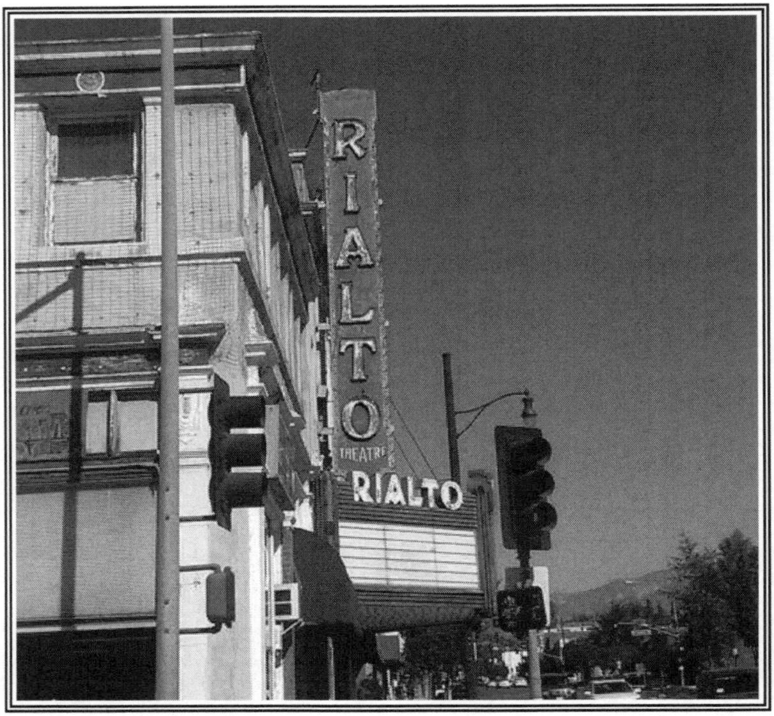

RIALTO
LOST BURNING YOUTH

"Tron"

1982

A world inside
the computer
where man
has never been.
Never before now.
TRON

This was hands down my favorite movie as a child. It still continues to be one of my all-time favorites today. When I heard there was a sequel coming out in 2010 I was one of the first ones in line opening day to see the movie.

“Tron” centers on Kevin Flynn (played by one of my favorite actors Jeff Bridges). Flynn is a software engineer who worked at one time for a company called ENCOM. His ideas were stolen by Ed Dillinger who in time became the head of the company.

Flynn no longer works for the company. He runs an arcade called “Flynn's.” He spends his free time trying to prove Dillinger stole his ideas by hacking into the mainframe of ENCOM. Flynn is stopped every time by the Master Control Program (MCP) which is an artificial intelligence created by Dillinger.

The MCP tells Dillinger of plans to take over outside mainframes. He is after such computers as the Kremlin and the Pentagon. Dillinger wants to stop it but the MCP threatens to expose him for stealing Flynn's games if he does anything.

Lora (who is Flynn's ex-girlfriend) and Alan (Lora's new boyfriend) tell Flynn that Dillinger knows about his hacking. He convinces them to sneak him in to get a higher security clearance. He is trying to get Alan's security program "Tron" into the system. The MCP uses a laser to digitize Flynn bringing him into the mainframe. Flynn learns that all programs look like the humans who created them. They call their creators "users."

The MCP and his assistant a program named Sark rule over the programs and attempt to get them to renounce their belief in the users. They force them to play games against each other where the loser is destroyed. Flynn meets Tron and Ram and the three escape into the mainframe during a game. When Ram dies after being wounded Flynn finds out that as a user he can manipulate the digital world.

Flynn, Tron and Yori (who looks like Lora) attempt to destroy the MCP. Tron communicates with Alan through an input/output junction and receives instructions. Flynn and Yori are captured by Sark and left to die on a ship.

Flynn keeps the ship intact while Sark reaches the core of the MCP on a shuttle with captured programs. Tron confronts Sark and critically injures him. The MCP tries to consume the captive programs but fails because he transfers all of his powers to Sark.

Tron tries to break through the shield of the MCP. Flynn throws himself into the MCP and distracts it so that Tron can penetrate a gap in its shield. Tron throws his disc into the MCP destroying it and Sark.

Programs once again start to communicate with their users. Flynn is sent back to the real world to the same computer terminal he was at originally. A printer begins to print out the evidence that Dillinger stole his work.

The next day Dillinger arrives in his office to see the MCP deactivated and proof of his theft on the computer screen. Flynn takes over as the head of ENCOM and is greeted getting off a helicopter by Lora and Alan.

On the next page is the one place I have been to from this movie. It is the building used as “Flynn's Arcade.” The building (which is actually a restaurant) looks exactly the same as it did in the movie.

The building is located at 9543 Culver Blvd. In Culver City. Parking can be a bit tricky but you can park a block or two away and the area is beautiful for walking.

CAMERA SUPPLY CO.
PHOTO
SUPPLIES
PHOTOGRAPHY
FLYNN'S

The Historic Pacific Theater in Hollywood Actress Carol Burnett was fired from here and told she would never make it. Her star now sits on the Walk of Fame right in front of the entrance. It is located at 6433 Hollywood Blvd.

"Wes Craven's New Nightmare"

1994

This film (which I must say is my mom's favorite of the series) follows Freddy Krueger into the real world. Heather Langenkamp who appears under her real name lives in Los Angeles with her son Dylan and her husband Chase. She is very popular because of her role as Nancy Thompson in the Nightmare series.

The movie starts with a nightmare where the family is attacked by Freddy's claw. In the dream Chase is working on a new nightmare movie and two of his helpers are killed. An earthquake wakes her up and she finds a cut on Dylan exactly where he was cut in her dream. She tries to ignore the possibility.

Heather has been getting calls from an obsessed fan who quotes a nursery rhyme in Freddy's voice. This comes as she meets with New Line Cinema and is asked to play Nancy again in a new movie. She finds out that Chase has been working on it without her knowledge.

Upon returning home she finds Dylan watching her original movie almost in a trance. He screams at her as he comes out of it. She calls Chase and he agrees to rush home. The two men who were killed in the dream never showed up for work.

On his way home Chase is attacked by Freddy's claw

when he falls asleep. He is killed when he crashes his truck. His death causes more trouble for Dylan. Heather's Nightmare co-star John Saxon shares his concerns. He suggests she seek medical treatment for Dylan and herself after she has a nightmare at her husband's funeral where Freddy was trying to take Dylan.

Dylan becomes increasingly paranoid of Freddy even though he has never watched the movies. Wes Craven suggests that Freddy is an evil entity who is drawn to his movies. Now that the series is done the entity wants to be Freddy and has focused on her as if she were Nancy. Robert Englund (who played Freddy) seems to have a mysterious knowledge of this new Freddy.

Heather takes Dylan to a hospital where the nurse keeps Dylan, suspecting abuse in the home. When Heather goes home to get his stuffed dinosaur, the babysitter (named Julie) tries to stop Dylan from being sedated. When he is sedated he falls asleep which allows Freddy to murder Julie.

Dylan sleep walks out of the hospital without staff realizing it. Freddy taunts him trying to draw him into traffic, as Heather chases Dylan across the freeway. She follows him all the way back to her home.

When she gets home she realizes that John Saxon is acting

as if he were her father from the movie (Don Thompson). Heather embraces her role as Nancy which allows Freddy to enter the real world. Freddy takes Dylan back to his world.

Heather finds a trail of sleeping pills and follows it to Freddy's world. Heather and Dylan fight Freddy eventually pushing him into an oven. This destroys the evil.

Heather and Dylan come back to the real world and find a screenplay of the film they are in. There is an inscription from Wes Craven thanking her for defeating Freddy and playing Nancy one more time. Dylan asks if it's a story. Heather says it is and reads it to her son as the movie ends.

On the next page is the one location from this movie that I have been to. It is the house that was used as Heather's house in the movie. The house looks exactly as it did in the movie with no differences that I could notice. The address is 5132 Calvin Avenue in Tarzana. **This is a private residence so please respect their privacy and do not trespass.**

*One of the great benefits of "Hunting Hollywood" is running into a show being filmed, such as this episode of **"Criminal Minds"** being filmed at Union Station in Downtown Los Angeles.*

"WarGames"

1983

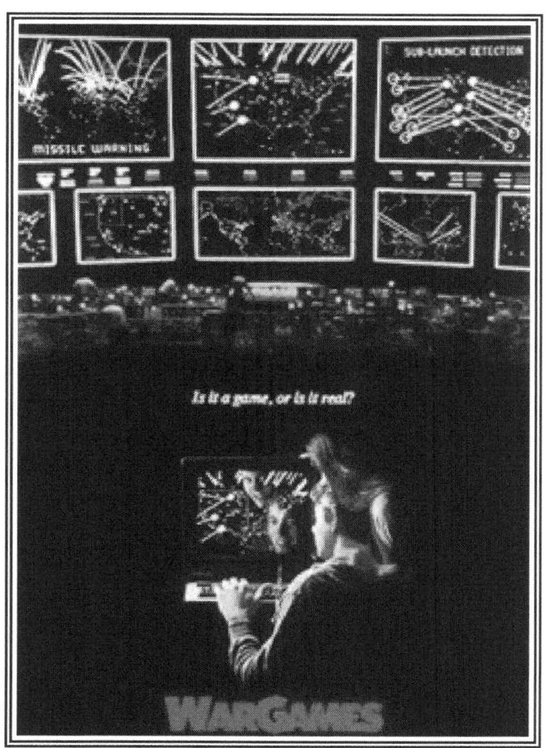

Engineers at NORAD are convinced that command of missile silos should be maintained through automation. Control is given over to a NORAD supercomputer named WOPR. It is programmed to continuously run military simulations and to learn over time.

Matthew Broderick plays David Lightman, a teenage hacker. When he receives a failing grade he hacks into the computer to change his grade and the grade of his friend Jennifer (played by the wonderful Ally Sheedy). In my opinion she is the greatest actress of the 1980's.

While dialing every number in Sunnyvale, California to find computer games. An unnamed computer intrigues David. He finds computer games like chess and checkers, as well as Chemical Warfare and Global Thermonuclear War.

His friends tell him about backdoor passwords and suggest he find the Falken from the game "Falcan's Maze." David finds out that a man named Stephen Falken was an artificial intelligence researcher. David guesses successfully that Falken's dead son's name Joshua is the password.

What David doesn't realize is that the phone number in Sunnyvale connects to the WOPR (also known as Joshua) at Cheyenne Mountain. He begins a game of Thermonuclear War and was playing as the Soviet Union. The computer simulation convinces the men at NORAD that actual missiles from the Soviets were inbound. They defuse the situation but Joshua continues the simulation to win.

While NORAD is on the verge of retaliating and starting World War 3, David finds out about the situation on the news. The FBI arrests him and takes him to NORAD. He realizes Joshua is behind the series of events but fails to convince leaders and faces prison.

David escapes NORAD by joining a tourist group and travels to the island near Oregon where Falken lives. David and Jennifer convince a despondent Falken to return to NORAD. Joshua stages a Soviet first strike and NORAD prepares to respond, believing it is real.

Falken, David and Jennifer convince NORAD to not respond but to wait out the attack. Joshua tries to respond itself by triggering a mass launch. They attempt to log in and cancel the launch but are unable. Falken and David convince the computer to play a game of tic-tac-toe against itself.

The computer reaches a series of ties which leads it to learn the concept of the unwinnable game. Obtaining the codes it needs, the computer runs through a series of nuclear matches and realizes they end in stalemate. The computer learns the concept of mutually assured destruction and realizes the only way to win is not to play. Joshua then offers to play a nice game of chess and releases control of the missiles and NORAD systems.

I have been to one location from this movie. On the next page is David's house from the movie. The house is almost completely unchanged from the movie and is absolutely beautiful. The address is 333 South Arden Blvd. In the Hancock Park area of Los Angeles. **This is a private residence so please respect their privacy and do not trespass.**

Santa Anita Park *located at 285 West Huntington Drive in Arcadia has a rich history in horseracing as well as films. Movies such as "A Day at the Races" with the Marx brothers, and "The Story of Seabiscuit" with Shirley Temple were filmed here.*

"Rebel Without a Cause"

1955

This movie (starring James Dean) is a classic and must see. This movie really defined the tough guy persona. It focuses on 17 year old Jim Stark who moves to Los Angeles with his parents.

Jim is taken to the police station for public drunkenness. His family troubles come out when they show up to bail him out. His parents fight a lot; his father tries to defend him but usually loses the arguments. His father's lack of moral strength troubles Jim.

Jim tries to conform to his peers but gets into a dispute with Buzz who is a bully. He makes friends such as John Plato who looks up to Jim. John's father left the family. The two first meet in the jail when Jim is taken in.

Jim also meets Judy played by the beautiful Natalie Wood. Judy was in the police station that night for being out alone after dark. She is not very impressed with Jim at first.

Jim goes with his school on a field trip to the Griffith Observatory. At the Observatory a group slashes his tire and Buzz challenges him to a knife fight. He doesn't want to take part in the fight until he is teased by the gang.

He takes part and wins the fight. He is later challenged to race stolen cars toward a cliff. This turns tragic as Buzz goes over the cliff because his leather jacket became stuck preventing him from jumping out.

Jim tells his parents and they urge him not to go to the police. He becomes angry and storms out of the house. Buzz's friends see Jim try to go to the police and they decide to hunt him down. They begin to harass his family and Plato to find him.

Plato finds Jim and Judy at an abandoned mansion. They act out a fantasy family while at the mansion. The gang finds them and Plato shoots one of them as well as firing at Jim and a police officer.

Plato hides in the Observatory which becomes surrounded by police. Jim and Judy go inside and convince him to give Jim the gun. Jim takes the bullets from the gun; Plato goes out of the Observatory and charges the police pulling out his gun. Before Jim can yell that he took the bullets Plato is shot and killed.

Plato was wearing Jim's jacket which lead his parents who arrive at the scene to believe that Jim was killed. When they realize Jim isn't dead, his dad promises to be a stronger father for him. Jim then introduces his parents to Judy.

On the next page is the one location that I have been to from this movie and that is inside the Griffith Observatory. In the picture I am standing in the same spot just inside the main entrance where James Dean was during the movie.

Rick Garland

Part 3:

Hunting Guide by City

Altadena:

Arleta:

Beverly Hills:

Brentwood:

Burbank:

Canyon Country:

Century City:

City Of Industry:

Culver City:

Downtown Los Angeles:

Fresno:

Hollywood:

Los Angeles:

About the Author

Rick Garland is co-founder at The March of Truth, an evangelistic and teaching ministry. His ministry website is marchoftruth.org. To reach Rick at his personal website please go to rickgarland.com. Rick and his wife Amy reside in Bakersfield, CA.